Daily Discoveries
for July

Thematic Learning Activities for
EVERY DAY

Written by Elizabeth Cole Midgley

Illustrated by Jennette Guymon-King

Teaching & Learning Company

1204 Buchanan St., P.O. Box 10

IL 62321-0010

This book belongs to

_____

Several of the activities in this book involve preparing, tasting and sharing food items. We urge you to be aware of any food allergies or restrictions your students may have and to supervise these activities diligently. All food-related suggestions are identified with this allergy-alert symbol: ⚠

Please note: small food items (candies, raisins, cereal, etc.) can also pose a choking hazard.

Cover art by Jennette Guymon-King

Copyright © 2006, Teaching & Learning Company

ISBN 13: 978-1-57310-485-2
ISBN 10: 1-57310-485-X

Printing No. 987654321

Teaching & Learning Company
1204 Buchanan St., P.O. Box 10
Carthage, IL 62321-0010

At the time of publication every effort was made to insure the accuracy of the information included in this book. However, we cannot guarantee that agencies and organizations mentioned will continue to operate or maintain these current locations.

Table of Contents

Dear Teacher or Parent,

Due to the stimulus of a high-tech world, parents and teachers are often faced with the challenge of how to capture the attention of a child and create an atmosphere of meaningful learning opportunities. Often we search for new ways to meet this challenge and help young people transfer their knowledge, skills and experiences from one area to another. Subjects taught in isolation can leave a feeling of fragmentation. More and more educators are looking for ways to be able to integrate curriculum so that their students can fully understand how things relate to each other.

The Daily Discoveries series has been developed to that end. The premise behind this series has been, in part, the author's educational philosophy: anything can be taught and absorbed by others in a meaningful way, depending upon its presentation.

In this series, each day has been researched around the history of a specific individual or event and has been developed into a celebration or theme with integrated curriculum areas. In this approach to learning students draw from their own experience and understanding of things, to a level of processing new information and skills.

The Daily Discoveries series is an almanac-of-sorts, 12 books (one for each month) that present a thematically based curriculum for grades K-6. The series contains hundreds and hundreds of resources and ideas that can be a natural springboard to learning. These ideas have been used in the classroom and at home, and are fun as well as educationally sound. The activities have been endorsed by professors, teachers, parents and, best of all, by children.

The Daily Discoveries series can be used in the following ways for school or home:
- to develop new skills and reinforce previous learning
- to create a sense of fun and celebration every day
- as tutoring resources
- as enrichment activities that can be used as time allows
- for family fun activities

Sincerely,

Elizabeth

Elizabeth Cole Midgley

Picnic Day
July 1

Setting the Stage

• Display a red-and-white checked picnic tablecloth as a background for this bulletin board idea. Students can draw ants for a border. They can write favorite summer activities (on paper plates) to display against the tablecloth backdrop with the caption: "Summer Can Be a Real Picnic!"

• Purchase tiny plastic black ants at a novelty store and place them on the floor leading into your classroom. You may prefer to copy ants on page 12, cut them out and tape them on the floor and on objects with clear tape.

• Display a picnic basket surrounded by literature about picnics.

• Construct a semantic web with words your students think of when you say the word *picnic*.

• Invite anyone who has an ant colony to bring it to school so your class can observe the ants in action.

Literary Exploration

Aardvark's Picnic by Jon Higham
Ant by David Hawcock
Antics by Cathi Hepworth
Ants Are Fun by Mildred Myrick
The Bear's Picnic by Stan Berenstain
The Bear's Water Picnic by John Yeoman
Before the Picnic by Yoriko Tsutsui
A Change of Plans by Alan Benjamin
Claude Has a Picnic by Dick Gackenback
Ernest and Celestine's Picnic by Gabrielle Vincent
Grandmother Lucy Goes on a Picnic by Joyce Wood
The Greatest Picnic in the World by Anna Grossnickle Hines
Having a Picnic by Sarah Garland
Helen the Hungry Bear by Marilyn MacGregor
How Do Ants Know When You're Having a Picnic? by Joanne Settel
July by James Stevenson
Little Bunny's Picnic by Michelle Cartlidge
Marmalade's Picnic by Lindy Wheeler
Mr. Bear's Picnic by Debi Gliori
Nicky's Picnic by Harriet Ziefert
On a Picnic by Judy Delton
Once We Went on a Picnic by Aileen Fisher
Picnic by Emily Arnold McCully
The Picnic by Ruth Brown

Literary Exploration continued

The Picnic by Kady Denton
A Picnic Hurrah! by Franz Brandenberg
Picnic Pandemonium by M. Christina Butler
Picnic with Piggins by Jane Yolen
The Rattlebang Picnic by Margaret Mahy
A Ripping Day for a Picnic by Keith DuQuette
Two Bad Ants by Chris Van Allsburg

Language Experience

• Let your students brainstorm words they can think of with the word *ant* in them (*anticipate, plant, slant, participant,* etc.).

Writing Experience

• Let students write recipes for perfect picnic lunches. See reproducible on page 13.

The Perfect Picnic

Math Experience

- Use small plastic ants as math manipulatives for counting, addition and subtraction practice or use the ant patterns on page 12.

- If you are eating at a picnic table, your students might want to measure the area and perimeter of the table.

Science/Health Experience

- At this time of year as we make plans to celebrate America's independence, we are reminded of the early colonists. Ants also live in colonies and are certainly a part of America! They have been a part of our picnics from the very beginning. Study ants and their habitat.

8

Music/Dramatic Experience
• Have students sing "The Ants Go Marching."

The ants go marching three by three....

• Borrow the sound recording of "Ants" by Joe Scruggs from a local library.

Physical/Sensory Experience
• After your class picnic, save some time for students to play on playground swings, slides, etc.

Arts/Crafts Experience
• Students can make ants by attaching pipe cleaner legs and antennae to an egg carton body. They can glue on wiggly eyes or draw them.

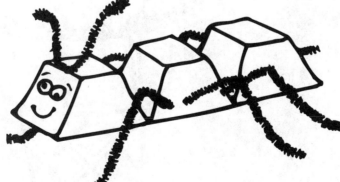

• Let students decorate a plain tablecloth with markers for a personalized class tablecloth.

Extension Activities

⚠ For a culminating activity, have a picnic! Serve food on a skewer (meat, fruit and vegetables). Even dessert can be placed on a skewer (soft cookies, marshmallows and fruit). Or you can tell students ahead of time to each bring a sack lunch for today.

⚠ Here's a creative picnic idea. Serve tuna salad (with an ice cream scoop) in ice cream cones. Be sure to keep the tuna salad very cold in a cooler before serving.

Extension Activities continued

⚠ Your students can make Hot Dog Hot-Rod Cars! Have each one carefully insert two small wooden skewers through either end of a hot dog in a bun. Then they stick four carrot slices on the skewers for wheels. Encourage them to observe the speed limit while they're eating!

⚠ Have students make "Ants on a Log" for a healthy treat. They spread peanut butter on a piece of celery and add raisins (ants) on top.

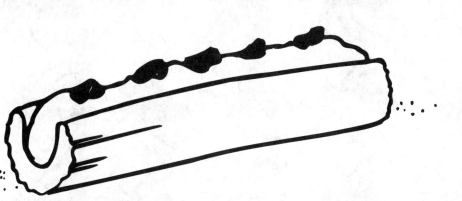

Follow-Up/Homework Idea

• Students can suggest their families have picnics for dinner tonight, even if its only in their backyards.

11

Picnic Day
Picnic Day
Picnic Day

12

The Perfect Picnic

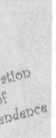

Declaration of Independence Day

July 2

Setting the Stage

• Display a copy of the Declaration of Independence surrounded by patriotic symbols and related literature.

Historical Background

The Continental Congress approved the Declaration of Independence on this day in 1776 in Philadelphia, Pennsylvania.

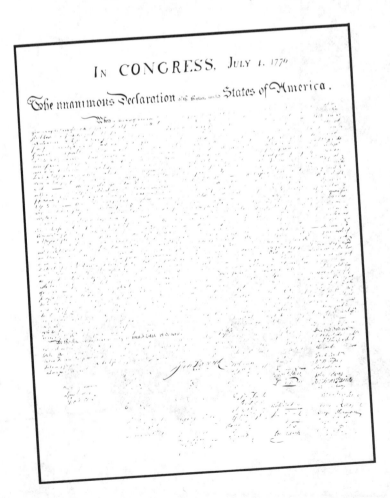

TLC10485 Copyright © Teaching & Learning Company, Carthage, IL 62321-0010

Literary Exploration

Ben Franklin by Ingri d'Aulaire
The Declaration of Independence by Dennis B. Fradin
The Declaration of Independence by R. Conrad Stein
Meet Ben Franklin by Maggi Scarf
Our Declaration of Independence by Jay Schleifer
Pass the Quill, I'll Write a Draft by Robert M. Quackenbush
Story of the Declaration of Independence by Norman Richards
Thomas Jefferson by Charles Patterson
Will You Sign Here, John Hancock? by Jean Fritz

Language Experience

• Divide students into teams and have a vocabulary scavenger hunt with some unfamiliar words from the Declaration of Independence. (Examples: self-evident, endowed, inalienable, pursuit)

Writing Experience

• Let students write their own "declarations of independence" proclaiming their desire for more freedom, such as staying up later or getting more privileges.

• Though Thomas Jefferson wrote the Declaration of Independence, some of his original words were changed by Benjamin Franklin to make it clearer. Have students write how they feel about being Americans, then exchange papers and "edit" one another's writing.

Social Studies Experience

- Study the events leading up to the writing of the Declaration of Independence.

- Let students research Thomas Jefferson to find out how he was qualified to write America's most important historic document. Have them share their findings with the class.

- Study the history of Independence Hall in Philadelphia, Pennsylvania, where the Declaration of Independence was accepted. What other historic event took place there?

- Amazingly, the original Declaration of Independence is on display for everyone to see in Washington, D.C. Have students research where it can be seen and how many people view it every year.

Music/Dramatic Experience

- Play patriotic musical selections in the background while students work.

- Let students work in pairs or small groups to write and perform raps about the Declaration of Independence.

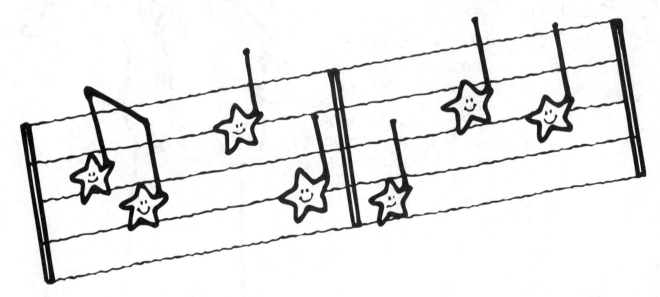

Arts/Crafts Experience

- Encourage students to draw pictures of Thomas Jefferson writing the Declaration of Independence. Tell them that he spent 17 days working on it, wanting it to be perfect, knowing how important it was. Challenge them to show that in their drawings.

- Let students design postage stamps that commemorate the writing of the Declaration of Independence.

Extension Activities

- Invite your school principal to come and read the Declaration of Independence (or excerpts from it) to your students.

- Let your class share their patriotism with others. Have them dress in red, white and blue to visit a center for senior citizens in the area. Ask good readers to read excerpts from the Declaration of Independence and have the class sing patriotic songs such as "America the Beautiful" and "Yankee Doodle."

Follow-Up/Homework Idea

- Encourage students to talk with their families about how they feel about living in a free country. Who should they thank for their freedom?

Idaho Statehood Day

July 3

Setting the Stage
• Display a bag of Idaho potatoes surrounded by pictures and books about Idaho.

Historical Background
Idaho became the 43rd state on this day in 1890.

Literary Exploration

America the Beautiful: Idaho by Zachary Kent
Idaho by Allan Carpenter
Idaho by Dennis Fradin
Idaho by Kathy Pelta
Idaho by Kathleen Thompson
Idaho in Words and Pictures by Dennis Fradin
Picture Book of Idaho by Bernadine Bailey
The Story of Idaho by Virgil Young

Language Experience

• Let students brainstorm words that have the long "o" sound as in *Idaho*.

• Challenge students to come up with descriptive phrases that rhyme with *Idaho*. (Example: Idaho, where potatoes grow)

• Have students research to find out where Idaho got its name. Have them share their findings with the class.

Writing Experience

• Idaho is known for its silver mining. Have students use their imagination to write stories about striking it rich at a silver mine in Idaho.

• Native Americans played an important role in the history of Idaho. Students can imagine they are Indians living in the Old West of Idaho and write about their adventures before the settlers moved in and took over.

Math Experience

• Let students play a relay game of Hot Potato Math. Cut out paper potato shapes and print a number on each one. Make two sets and put them in two baskets. Divide students into two teams. Set the potato baskets on a table and line up the teams about 20 feet away. At your signal the first student on each team runs to the basket and quickly grabs two "potatoes," then brings them back to you at the starting line. The student must add or multiply (your choice) the two numbers before the next student on the team can continue the game. If a student does not know the answer, he or she can choose a team member to help get the answer.

Science/Health Experience

• Let students grow Idaho potatoes in cups of water. Suspend the potato from the cup with toothpicks, submerging just the bottom half in the water.

Social Studies Experience

• Study the state of Idaho and the things that make it unique.

• Have students locate Idaho on a United States map and name the six states that border it.

• Let students research the Nez Perce Indians in Idaho, and their famous chief, Chief Joseph. What did he say when his people surrendered in the war of 1877?

• The Snake River is an important river in the history of Idaho. Study the part it played in the pioneers' westward trek on the Oregon Trail in the mid 1800s.

• Challenge students to find out why Idaho is called the Gem State.

Physical/Sensory Experience

• If possible, bring some gems (opals, garnets, etc.) to class for students to feel and examine.

20

Arts/Crafts Experience

• Let each student make an Idaho state flag.

• Idaho has one of the largest examples of Indian petroglyphs ever found. They are pictures drawn by Indians on lava rock. The pictures show a map of their seasonal travels and a battle fought 300-400 years ago between warring tribes. Let students draw petroglyphs, using stick-figure art, to tell about something that has happened to them.

• Idaho is known for its abundant wildlife and beautiful scenery. Let students work together to create a mural of Idaho's beauty. (Make sure they find out what birds, animals and flowers live in Idaho first.)

Extension Activities

⚠ Serve "spudnuts" (Doughnuts made with potatoes in them.), potato pancakes, potato bread or Tator Tots™ as a treat.

• Invite someone who has lived in or visited Idaho to visit your class to tell about it and show pictures.

Follow-Up/Homework Idea

• Students can ask their parents to serve Idaho potatoes for dinner tonight!

Idaho Statehood

Idaho Statehood

Idaho Statehood

Independence
Day

Independence
Day

Independence
Day

Independence Day

July 4

Setting the Stage

• Encourage everyone to dress in red, white and blue. Display patriotic symbols around related literature to gather excitement about the day.

• Construct a semantic web with facts your students know about Independence Day. List together additional things they would like to know.

Historical Background

Today is the day that the Continental Congress adopted and signed the Declaration of Independence. America celebrates its birthday on this day because on July 4, 1776, we declared we would no longer be ruled by Great Britain.

Literary Exploration

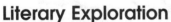

America's Birthday: Fourth of July by Tom Schactman

Fireworks, Picnics and Flags: The Story of Fourth of July Symbols by James Cross Giblin

Fourth of July by Barbara Joosse

The Fourth of July by Janet McDonnell

Fourth of July by Mary Kay Phelan

Fourth of July Bear by Kathryn Lasky

The Fourth of July Story by Alice Dalgliesh

Henrietta's Fourth of July by Sydney Hoff

Henry's Fourth of July by Holly Keller

Hurray for Fourth of July by Wendy Watson

It's the Fourth of July by Stan Hoig

My First Fourth of July Book by Harriet Hodgson

Our Country's Story by Frances Cavanah

Language Experience

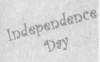

• Let students list and discuss the freedoms they enjoy in America.

• Have students think of adjectives to describe how they feel on July 4th.

Writing Experience

• Give students an opportunity to write about why they are glad to be Americans. See reproducible on page 27.

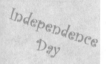

Social Studies Experience

• Learn about the historical events leading up to July 4th, and the results.

• Begin a unit of study on patriotism. Who were the patriots who fought for Americas freedom? Who are the patriots today?

• Discuss the rights and responsibilities of freedom.

Music/Dramatic Experience

• Sing "America the Beautiful" and other patriotic songs.

Physical/Sensory Experience

• Have a 4th of July Patriotic Parade. Let students bring musical instruments or make homemade ones. Have them wave American flags and play their instruments as they march around the school.

Arts/Crafts Experience

• Students can make fireworks pictures by dropping a teaspoon of tempera paint onto art paper, then blowing it with a straw across the paper.

Extension Activities

⚠ Serve red, white and blueberry sundaes! Students can add strawberry topping and fresh or frozen blueberries to vanilla ice cream.

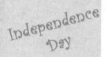

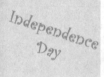

Values Education Experience

• Print on the board: *Freedom isn't free.* Ask students what that means. Who can we thank for the freedom we enjoy?

Follow-Up/Homework Idea

• Students can decorate their bikes with red, white and blue crepe paper, weaving it in and out of the wheel spokes. They can ride in a neighborhood parade with their friends to celebrate freedom.

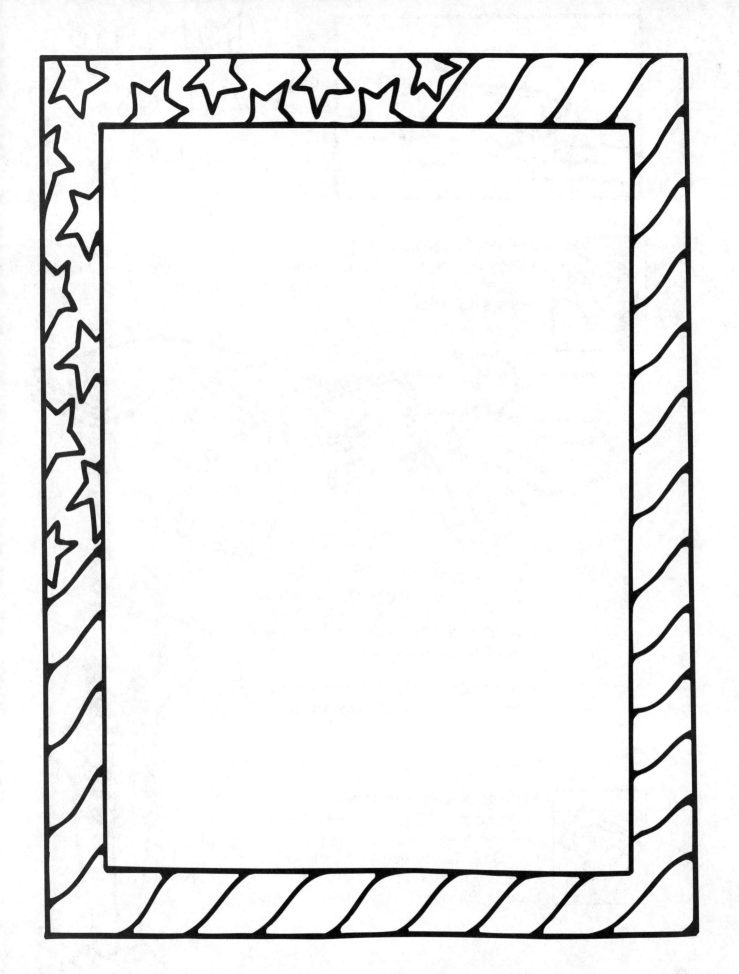

Bathing Beauties Day

July 5

Setting the Stage
• Display bathing suits and swimming apparatus (goggles, snorkels, towels) around related literature to get students excited about the day's activities.

• Encourage summer reading with copies of book covers on a wavy blue paper background and the caption: "Dive into a Good Book Today!"

• Construct a semantic web with facts your students know about swimming.

Historical Background
On this day in 1946, Louis Reard shocked everyone with the invention of his new bathing suit, the bikini. Today every kind of bathing suit can be seen at beaches around the world as people soak up the sun and swim.

Literary Exploration

Cannonball Chris by Jean Marzollo
Last One in Is a Rotten Egg by Leonard Kessler
Let's Go Swimming! by Shigeo Watanabe
Let's Go Swimming with Mr. Sillypants by M.K. Brown
Lulu Goes Swimming by Susanne Strub
Maisy Goes Swimming by Lucy Cousins
Making Waves: The Story of the American Swimsuit by Lena Lencek
Safety First: Water by Cynthia Klingel
Safety in the Sand by Marcia Leonard
Swimming Hole by Jerrold Beim
Swimming Is for Me by Lowell Dickmeyer

Language Experience

• Let students brainstorm words that rhyme with *swim*.

Writing Experience

• Students can write "at the beach" stories using these story starters:
   As I was walking along the beach, I suddenly saw . . .
   When I saw a child fall off a raft into deep water, I . . .
   Coming down the beach was a person wearing the strangest swim
      suit I had ever seen. It was . . .
   A day at the beach is always fun, especially when . . .

• Have students write newspaper stories with headlines about an exciting event at the beach. Remind them to answer the five questions every news story includes: Who? What? When? Where? Why?

Science/Health Experience
• Review swimming safety.

• Discuss buoyancy. Why do plump people often float in the water more easily than thin people? Why is it easier to float in the ocean than in a lake?

Social Studies Experience
• Study the history of swim wear. Show pictures of how it has changed over the years.

• Ask students to share their favorite places to swim and explain why these places are good.

Music/Dramatic Experience
• Play some Beach Boys music and let students pantomime swimming and surfing to it.

Arts/Crafts Experience

• Let students work together in pairs or small groups to create swimming collages. They can draw water on poster board, then glue on pictures of fish, swimmers, surfers, etc., they have cut from magazines. Then they can cover the posters with blue cellophane to give them an underwater feel.

Physical/Sensory Experience

• Check with a local YMCA or high school to get permission to use their pool to take your class swimming. Be sure to watch students carefully since some may not know how to swim. Ask for parent volunteers to help.

Extension Activities

• Invite a member of the high school swim team to come and talk about why he or she enjoys swimming and to give suggestions for becoming a better swimmer.

Follow-Up/Homework Idea

• Students can go swimming with their families. Swimming is a great way for families to play together.

Bathing
Beauties

Bathing
Beauties

Bathing
Beauties

Getting to Know You Day

July 6

Setting the Stage

- Begin an ongoing "Spotlight" bulletin board to display pictures, memorabilia (trophies, stuffed animals) to highlight students in your class. Enlist parental support, letting them come and talk about their children when they are featured so your class can get to know them better. Give each parent a large, yellow paper sun to fill up with pictures or items to represent the child and display it on the bulletin board all week (or until it's the next student's turn). For added fun, place tiny electric lights all around the board to make it stand out! See sun pattern on page 38.

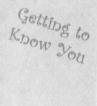

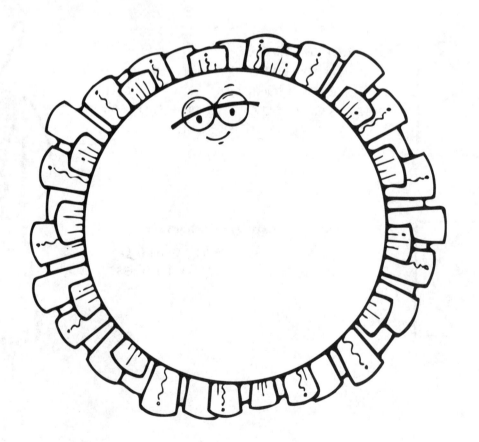

32

Literary Exploration

All About Me by Melanie Rice
I Like You, If You Like Me by Myra Cohn Livingston
My Book About Me by Dr. Suess
Tell Me About Yourself: How to Interview by D.L. Mabery
They Really Like Me! by Anna Grossnickle Hines

Language Experience

- Students can teach everyone the correct pronunciation of their names (avoiding mispronunciations) by printing their names with pronunciation marks where needed. They can use the pronunciation guide from a dictionary to figure out where syllables and accent marks go.

- Challenge students to come up with positive rhyming phrases to identify classmates. (Example: Annie Grundy, always sunny on Monday)

Writing Experience

- Reinforce descriptive writing with this activity. Ask students to each secretly pick someone in the room to describe in positive terms. (Example: This person is a boy. He has brown hair. He is wearing striped socks.) After students write their descriptive sentences, collect the papers. Have everyone stand. Read each descriptive sentence aloud. If the description does not fit them, they sit down. When only one student is still standing, it is the person described.

It's me!

Writing Experience continued

• Let students begin writing in journals of some kind. This is an excellent way for them to get to know themselves as they explore their feelings and process their experiences. Set aside some time each day or several times a week for students to continue their journal writing throughout the year.

• Let students write descriptive words about themselves in balloons. See reproducible on page 39.

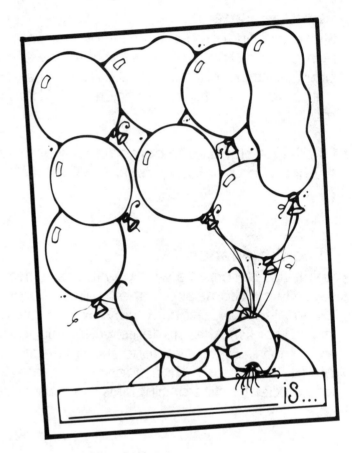

• Students will enjoy writing about one of these story starters:

I feel happiest when . . .
One of the best things I know about myself is . . .
It would be great if someone would give me . . .
Something I wish I could change is . . .
I think I look best when . . .
When I make a mistake, I feel . . .
I'm the kind of person who . . .
I think I'm especially good at . . .
The thing I am most proud of is . . .
I wish someone could help me with . . .
I really, really like . . .

34

Math Experience

- Get students involved in graphing activities. Make a large class graph with descriptive phrases such as: I have more than one brother, I have a cat, I have a dog, etc. Students can color a square for each item that fits their circumstances.

Social Studies Experience

- Talk about getting to know each other and the kinds of behavior that encourage us to be friendly. Discuss how to make friends.

Music/Dramatic Experience

- Check out Hap Palmer's sound recording of *Getting to Know Myself*.

- Read the book, *Tell Me About Yourself: How to Interview* by D.L. Mabery, to explore the basics of conducting an interview. Then let students interview one another with questions they have prepared. These can be shared in written or oral report form.

Physical/Sensory Experience

• Play Get-to-Know-You Bingo. The teacher tells everyone a category (favorite color, favorite hobby, number of sisters, etc.). Students write their favorite colors in whatever squares they choose. Then they write their other favorites and other information the teacher asks for. When the card is filled, the game begins. The teacher may call out "orange" or "jumping rope." Students who have those, cover the square with a raisin or jelly bean. The winner is the student who first completes a line going up, down or diagonally across. See patterns on page 40.

• Have a People Scavenger Hunt! As a class, brainstorm a list of things that tell about a person (takes music lessons, has a pet or has a collection). Give each student a list. Let them search for someone who fits each category and have that person sign the list. The first person to find someone in the class for each category is the winner!

• Here's a fun memory game! Each student writes his or her name on a piece of paper, then exchanges it with another student. As the exchange is being made, the students reveal a little about themselves to each other. After a few minutes, the students go back to their seats. Then one at a time, they introduce the new friend (with the information learned) to the rest of the class. This is a great way to help the class get to know shy students.

Arts/Crafts Experience
• Let students cut out magazine pictures of items that reflect their personalities and put them together in collages. They can glue the pictures on outlines of kids' bodies. Display the people collages around the room. See patterns on pages 41-42.

Values Education Experience
• Talk about having a feeling of unity and teamwork in the class. Enlist student support to help everyone feel valued and an important part of the class.

Follow-Up/Homework Idea
• Encourage students to tell their families about their classmates.

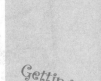

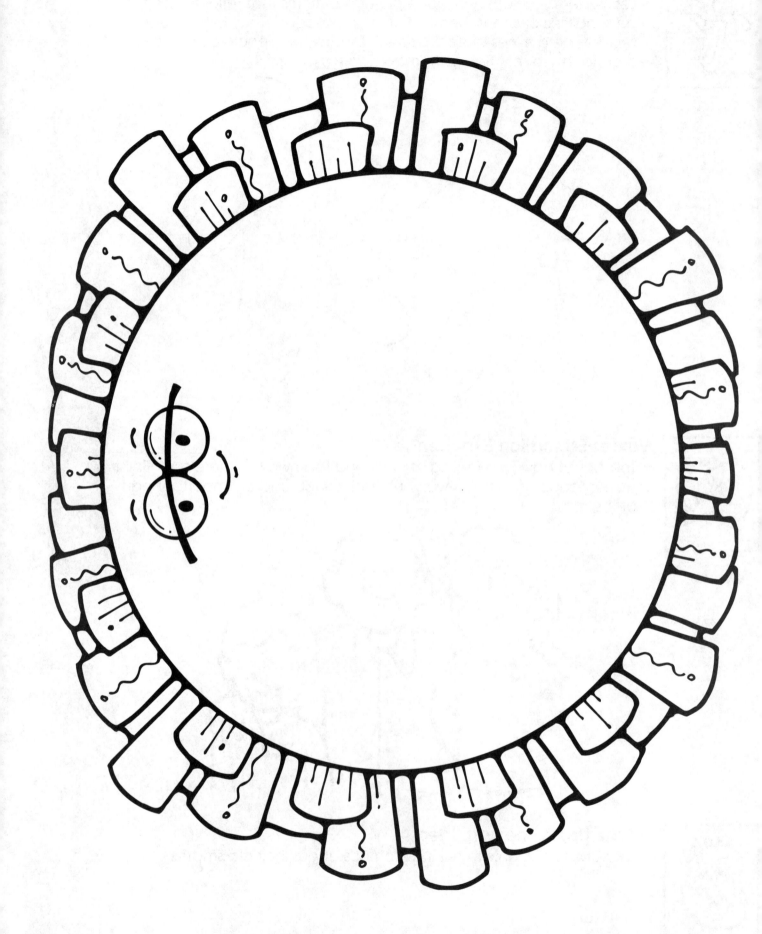

iS...

42

Fun with Puppets Day

July 7

Setting the Stage
• Display all kinds of puppets around related literature.

• Construct a semantic map or web with facts your students know (or would like to know) about puppetry.

Literary Exploration
Easy to Make Puppets by Frieda Gates
Easy to Make Puppets by Joyce Luckin
Finger Puppets: Easy to Make and Fun to Use by Laura Ross
I Can Make a Puppet by Mary Wallace
Jim Henson: From Muppet to Puppet by Geraldine Woods
Knowhow Book of Puppets by Violet Philpott
Make Amazing Puppets by Nancy Renfro
Making Easy Puppets by Shari Lewis
Plays for Puppet Performances by George Merten
Puppet Fun by Nellie McCaslin
Puppet Making by Chester Jay Alkema
Puppet Party by Goldie Chernoff
Puppet Plays from Favorite Stories by Lewis Mahlmann
Puppet Shows Made Easy by Nancy Renfro
Puppets by Gertrude Pels

Language Experience
• Gather finger plays or choral readings to involve students in a warm-up for the puppetry activities throughout the day.

Writing Experience

- Divide the class into cooperative learning groups and let them combine their efforts to write scripts for puppet plays to be performed later in the day. They can write scripts for *Goldilocks and the Three Bears* or *The Three Little Pigs* since patterns for both stories are provided on pages 48-52. You'll be amazed at different versions you get of the same stories!

Social Studies Experience

- Study the history of puppetry.

- Let interested students research famous puppeteers, such as Jim Henson or Shari Lewis. Have them share their findings with the rest of the class.

44

Music/Dramatic Experience

• Today wouldn't be complete without an actual puppet show! Let cooperative groups act out their puppet shows written earlier for the rest of the class.

• Let students design simple finger puppets to wear. They can use the finger puppets to sing songs or make announcements to the class.

GOLDILOCKS & THE THREE BEARS

Physical/Sensory Experience

• Teach your students the basics of manipulating a string puppet or hand puppet. If there aren't enough puppets to go around, let them take turns practicing.

Arts/Crafts Experience

• Borrow a book about puppet making from a local library and let students try it. They can make puppets from old socks, buttons and felt, or from construction paper glued to craft sticks or straws.

Arts/Crafts Experience continued

• Let students make paper bag puppets for *Goldilocks and the Three Bears* or stick puppets for *The Three Little Pigs*! They can take them home and put on puppet shows for their families! See Goldilocks and the Three Bears sack puppet patterns on pages 48-51 and the Three Little Pigs stick puppet patterns on page 52.

Extension Activities

- Take your class to a puppet show (professional or high school production) if you can. If not, watch a Muppets DVD together.

- Invite a local puppeteer to visit your class to talk about his or her work.

Values Education Experience

- Discuss how people are not like puppets, but are free to think and act for themselves. A puppet can always blame someone else for its actions, but we have to take responsibility for our own actions.

Follow-Up/Homework Idea

- Encourage students to take their puppets home and put on puppet shows for family members or young children in the neighborhood.

48

50

52

Liberty Bell Day

July 8

Liberty
Bell

Setting the Stage

• Display a picture of the Liberty Bell and other patriotic symbols around related literature.

• Construct a semantic web with facts your students know (or would like to know) about the Liberty Bell to help you structure your day.

Liberty
Bell

Historical Background

The Liberty Bell rang on this day in 1776 to summon people to come and hear the first public reading of the new Declaration of Independence. The bell was created in 1751 to celebrate the 50th anniversary of William Penn's 1701 Charter of Privileges, Pennsylvania's original constitution. Unfortunately it cracked and had to be recast in 1753. It cracked again when it was rung on George Washington's birthday in 1846 and was left as it was. It became an even bigger symbol of America after that time. It still hangs today in Independence Hall in Philadelphia, Pennsylvania.

Liberty
Bell

Liberty
Bell

Literary Exploration
The Story of the Liberty Bell by Natalie Miller

Language Experience
• Let students brainstorm as many words as they can that rhyme with the word *bell*.

Writing Experience
• Let students write the Liberty Bell's story from its own point of view.

• Have students write haiku poems about the Liberty Bell. A haiku poem has three unrhyming lines. The first and third lines have only five syllables each while the second line has seven syllables.

Example: The Liberty Bell—
America's cracked symbol
of a whole nation

Math Experience
• Have students use their math skills to figure out how old the Liberty Bell is. How old was it when it stopped working?

• Review telling time with younger students. Ring a small bell to tell the time. Have students draw hands on clocks to show the time you rang.

Science/Health Experience
• Study sound. Bring various sizes of bells for students to ring. Which ringing sounds are higher? Which are louder? Why? Why does a crack diminish the sound of a bell's ring?

Social Studies Experience

• Study the history of the Liberty Bell and its significance. Explain that it had to be kept hidden under a church floor in Allentown, Pennsylvania, during the British occupation of its native city of Philadelphia between 1777-1778.

• Have students research to find out how many times the bell malfunctioned and had to be fixed or recast. Why was it such a popular symbol in spite of its problems?

Music/Dramatic Experience

• Play patriotic music quietly in the background as students are involved in their projects today.

Arts/Crafts Experience

• Let students make Liberty Bells out of Styrofoam™ cups covered with aluminum foil. Insert a string with a jingle bell tied on the end. Pull it through a small hole in the base of the cup. Tie a knot in the string so it will not pull through the hole.

• Students can try sculpting bells from clay. Or give each student a small clay flowerpot, some string, a small stick and a jingle bell. They can tie the bell on one end of the string, they tie the stick to the string about three to four inches from the bell to hold it inside the pot. They pull the string through the hole in the base of the pot and hang it or attach another piece of stick to keep the handle from pulling through the hole.

Follow-Up/Homework Idea

• Encourage students to share what they learned about the Liberty Bell today with their families.

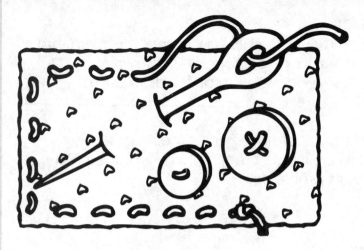

Sewing Day

July 9

Setting the Stage

• Display sewing materials and paraphernalia around related literature.

• Construct a semantic web with facts your students know or want to learn about sewing.

Historical Background

Today marks the birth of Elias Howe (born in 1819), the inventor of the lock stitching sewing machine.

Literary Exploration

The Brave Tailor by Dinah Anastasio
The Elves and the Shoemaker by Walt Disney
The Monster and the Tailor by Paul Galdone
Of Course You Can Sew! by Barbara Corrigan
Sam Johnson and the Blue Ribbon Quilt by Lisa Campell Ernst
Sewing by Hand by Christine Hoffman
The Sewing Machine by Beatrice Siegel

56

Language Experience

• Let students brainstorm other "ew" endings as in *sew*. Have them group the words by the sounds the "ew" makes.

Writing Experience

• Let students write a humorous story entitled, "This Will Keep You in Stitches!" See reproducible on page 60.

This will keep you in stitches!

• Students can make up their own fairy tales about a princess and a magic sewing machine that could make amazing things!

Math Experience

• Cut various lengths of thread and let students measure them in inches and in centimeters.

Social Studies Experience

- Review the history of the sewing machine. How did it make life easier especially for women?

- Ask interested students to do additional research on Elias Howe and what led to the invention of his sewing machine.

Sewing Day

Music/Dramatic Experience

- Let interested students act out a scene from the popular fairy tale, *The Elves and the Shoemaker.*

Sewing Day

Physical/Sensory Experience

- Provide fabric scraps, needles and thread and show students basic hand sewing techniques.

Sewing Day

Arts/Crafts Experience

- Let students make portable sewing kits to keep in their desks in case of an emergency such as a button popping off. Copy the pattern provided for each student on cardstock. Students cut out the cover and fold it like a matchbook cover. Then they cut out the second card with notches along the sides to hold thread and fit it inside the cover. Have them wrap four or five colors of thread around the notches. Using the dotted pattern, students cut out a small piece of material to hold a couple of needles and a safety pin. They staple the fabric piece and the thread card into the cover and staple them at the bottom. Then they can decorate the cover. See patterns on page 61.

See patterns on page 61.

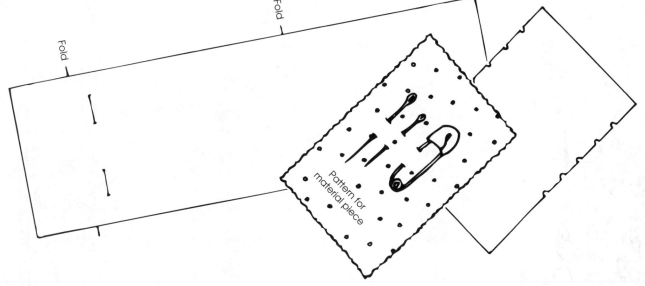

Fold

Fold

Pattern for material piece

Extension Activities

- Invite a tailor or seamstress to visit your class and talk about his or her work.

- Visit a sewing factory or tailor shop so your class can see what happens behind the scenes.

Values Education Experience

- Discuss how knowing basic skills such as sewing helps us become independent and self-reliant. What are some other useful skills everyone should acquire?

Pants
back
2

cut 2

Follow-Up/Homework Idea

- Encourage each student to volunteer to help Mom organize the family sewing kit. This will be good practice in categorizing.

Sewing Day

Sewing Day

Sewing Day

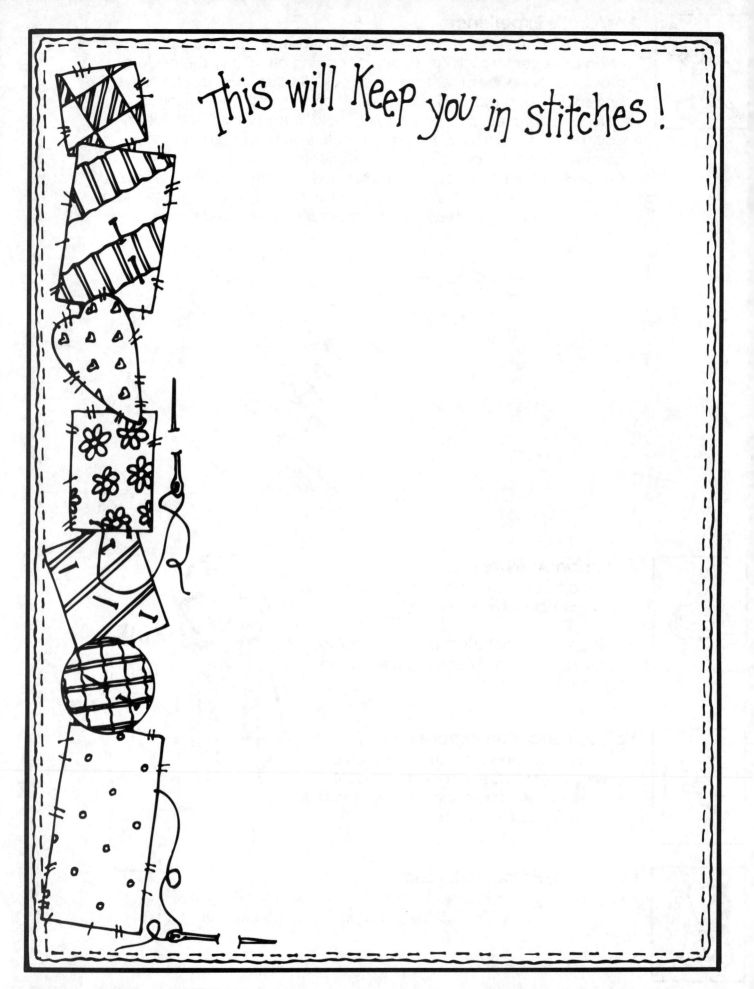

This will Keep you in stitches!

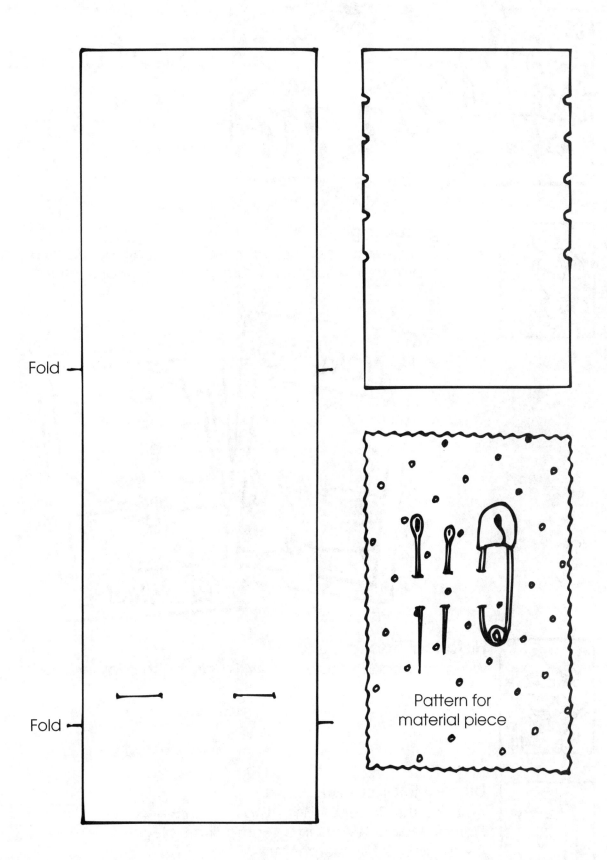

Fold

Fold

Pattern for
material piece

Wyoming Statehood

Wyoming Statehood Day

July 10

Setting the Stage

- Display travel posters and pamphlets (from a local travel agency) that represent the state of Wyoming around related literature.

Historical Background

Wyoming became America's 44th state on this day in 1890.

Literary Exploration

America the Beautiful: Wyoming by Ann Heinrichs
Picture Book of Wyoming by Bernadine Bailey
Wyoming by Allan Carpenter
Wyoming by Dennis Fradin
Wyoming by Carlienne Frisch
Wyoming by Kathleen Thompson
Wyoming in Words and Pictures by Dennis B. Fradin

Language Experience

• How many new words can your students make using the letters in *Wyoming*?

• Challenge students to research how Wyoming got its name, then report to the rest of the class.

Social Studies Experience

• Study the state of Wyoming and what makes it unique.

• Wyoming is home to Yellowstone, America's first national park. Let students research Yellowstone and share the information with the rest of the class.

Music/Dramatic Experience

• Borrow cowboy music recordings from a local library to play for your students.

• Let students wear cowboy hats and pretend to ride, rope and raise a ruckus, cowboy style!

Arts/Crafts Experience

• Let students make salt dough relief maps of the state of Wyoming.

• Beef is Wyoming's chief product so students can draw pictures of cattle grazing in Wyoming pastures.

Wyoming Statehood

Extension Activities

• Invite someone who has lived in or visited the state of Wyoming to share information, pictures or memorabilia with your class.

• Check out a movie of Yellowstone National Park from the library for your class to watch.

Wyoming Statehood

Follow-Up/Homework Idea

• Students can suggest that their families barbecue or go out for steak (Wyoming's chief product) tonight!

Wyoming Statehood

Wyoming Statehood

E.B. White's Birthday

July 11

Setting the Stage
• Display an array of E.B. White's books with pictures of mice, pigs, spiders, swans, etc., to gather excitement about today's activities.

Historical Background
American author E.B. White was born on this day in 1899. White received many distinguished awards during his long career for the contributions he made to children's literature.

Literary Exploration
Charlotte's Web by E.B. White
Stuart Little by E.B. White
Trumpet of the Swan by E.B. White

Language Experience
• Play the Clothesline Game (a variation of the Hangman game). Students try to avoid putting clothing items on the line, using wrong letters used. Let students try to guess what White's initials "E.B." stand for. (Elwyn Brooks)

E.B. White

E.B. White

E.B. White

Writing Experience

• The character in the book, *Stuart Little,* was inspired by a dream that E.B. White had. A mouse named Stuart became a member of the Little family. Ask each student to imagine that an animal comes to live with him or her and be part of the family. Let them write about their animal "sister or brother," telling some of their adventures. See reproducible on page 68.

My New Family Member

Social Studies Experience

• Let students do additional biographical research on E.B. White and share their findings with the rest of the class.

Music/Dramatic Experience

• Let students act out scenes from one of E.B. White's books. They can make masks to wear for the parts they play.

Arts/Crafts Experience

• Let students illustrate a scene from one of E.B. White's books.

• Students can draw swans on a lake with white crayon, then paint over it with black or dark blue watercolor. The white crayon swans will pop out for a fun *Trumpet of the Swan* scene.

Follow-Up/Homework Idea

• Encourage each student to check out one of E.B. White's books to take home and begin reading tonight.

My New Family Member

Space Day
July 12

Setting the Stage
• Display *Star Wars* and *Star Trek* memorabilia around related literature.

Historical Background
Since ancient times people have been wondering about space. Is there life out there? If so, what is it like? Writers and filmmakers have given us intriguing pictures of what life in outer space might be like. The amazing thing is that some of their imagined ideas have occasionally come true! Fortunately, most of them haven't!

Literary Exploration
Mystery of the Rebellious Robot by Mark Corcoran
Star Wars by Christopher Lampton
Star Wars C-3PO's Book About Robots by Joanne Ryder
Star Wars! The Making of the Movie by Larry Weinberg
Star Wars Questions and Answers Book by Dinah Moche

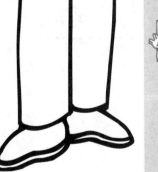

Language Experience
• Let students brainstorm words that have the "ar" sounds that *star* and *wars* have.

Science/Health Experience
• Review astronomy facts, such as the names and positions of the planets.

Space Day

Music/Dramatic Experience
• Borrow a music soundtrack of *Star Wars* or *Star Trek* to play quietly while students are working on their projects.

Space Day

Arts/Crafts Experience
• Students can draw their favorite *Star Wars* or *Star Trek* characters or creatures.

Space Day

Arts/Crafts Experience continued

• Let students work together to make a class robot from boxes, paper, paints and other craft materials. Anything goes when it comes to the size or shape of the robot! Let them use their imagination to decide what tasks the robot can perform. Be sure to give the robot a name.

RIGHTY
ROBOT

• Students can wear their own Vulcan ears (like Mr. Spock in *Star Trek*) throughout the day. Using the pattern, copy ears on light green cardstock for each student to cut out. Provide string to tie the ears around the top of the student's head and under the chin. See patterns on page 73.

Extension Activities

• Invite a representative from a local *Star Wars* or *Star Trek* fan club to come and share information or memorabilia with your class.

Follow-Up/Homework Idea

• Have students get permission to watch the night sky tonight to make observations. Perhaps they'll see a space ship or at least a falling star!

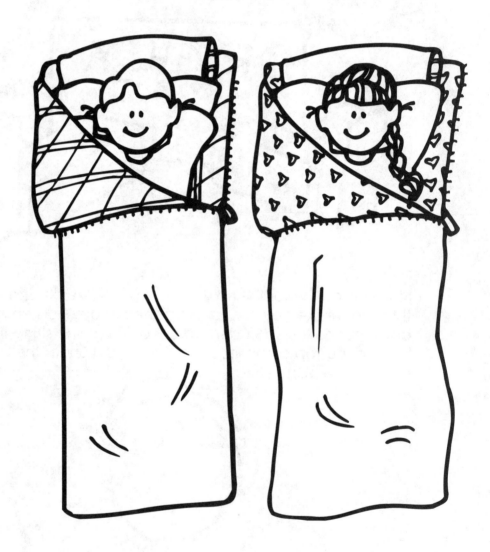

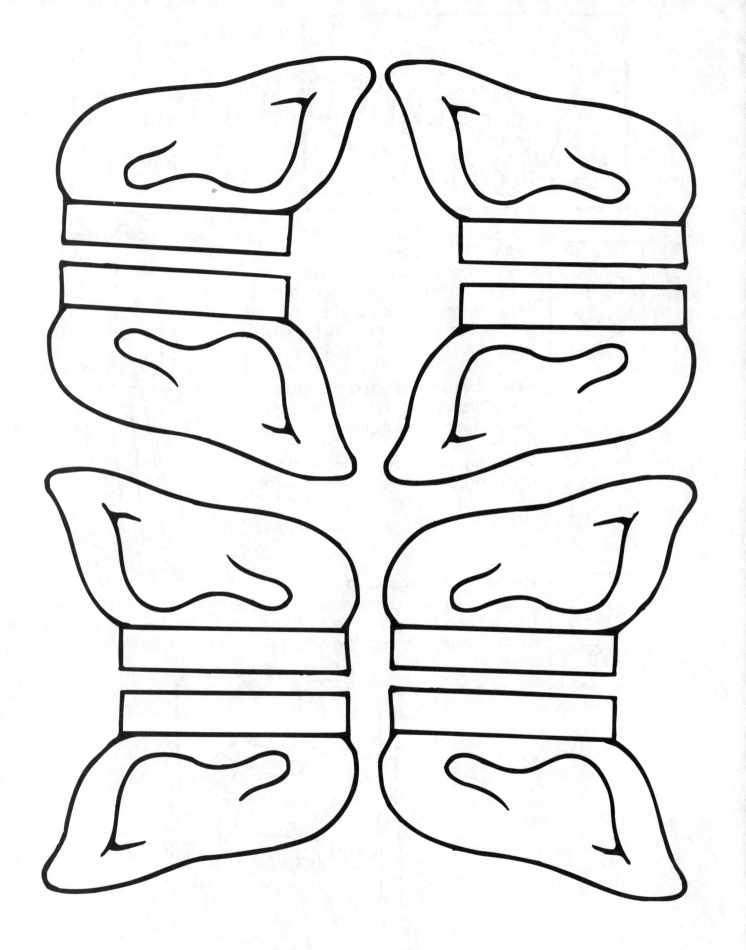

Roman
Ruins

Roman
Ruins

Roman
Ruins

Roman Ruins Day

July 13

Setting the Stage

• Display travel posters and brochures depicting Italy (especially Rome) from a local travel agency. These can be attractively displayed around related literature.

• Greet students dressed in a toga (a white top sheet and a belt), a laurel leaf crown and sandals!

• Construct a semantic web with facts your students know (or would like to know) about Rome, Italy.

Historical Background

Julius Caesar was born on this day in 100 B.C. He was a Roman general and statesman, very influential in his day. He became master of the Roman world, but was assassinated by a friend in 44 B.C.

Literary Exploration

Amzat and His Brothers: Three Italian Tales by Floriano Vecchi and Paula Fox

Ancient Rome by Charles Alexander Robinson

The Bronze Bow by Elizabeth George Speare

Count Your Way Through Italy by Jim Haskins

The Destruction of Pompeii by Mike Rosen

Everyday Life in Roman Times by Mike Corbishley

Grandfather's Rock: An Italian Folktale by Joel Strangis

How Would You Survive in Ancient Rome? by Anita Ganeri

Marc Anthony by Mary Kittredge

The Mysterious Giant of Barletta: An Italian Folktale by Tomie dePaola

Peppe the Lamplighter by Elisa Bartone

Petrosinella: A Neapolitan Rapunzel by Diane Stanley

The Roman Empire by Don Nardo

The Roman Empire by Jose Corte Salinas

Roman Numerals by David A. Adler

Roman People by Sarah Howarth

The Roman Stories by Robert Hull

The Roman World by Mike Corbishley

Silver at Night by Susan Campbell Bartoletti

Stega Nona by Tomie dePaola

Two Roman Mice by Marilyn Roach

Roman Ruins

Roman Ruins

Roman Ruins

Math Experience

• Teach your students the basics of the Roman Numeral System. Let them write their birth dates in Roman numerals.

Social Studies Experience

• Study briefly the rise and fall of the Roman Empire.

• Have students locate Rome, Italy on a world map. Talk about the extent of the Roman Empire during Julius Caesar's lifetime. Have students locate on the map the countries that became "Roman."

Arts/Crafts Experience

- Review great Italian artists, such as: Michelangelo, Leonardo da Vinci, Raphael and Donatello. Show samples of their work.

- Let students make their own laurel leaf crowns. Have them measure a piece of wire that wraps from ear to ear plus an additional four inches (to extend past the ears). They can cut leaves from green crepe paper and glue them to the wire in a variegated pattern. When it is dry, they can bend the wire to fit around their heads.

Extension Activities

⚠ Serve Little Caesar's Pizza™ and Orange Julius'™ (orange smoothie) for a fun treat!

Follow-Up/Homework Idea

- Before you say "Arrive derci" to your students, encourage them to ask their parents if they have any ancestors from Italy. If not, where did their ancestors live?

76

Treasure Island Day

July 14

Setting the Stage

• Create an island retreat area with a palm tree made of butcher paper and a background scene of blue waves and green grass or sand. A crate lying on its side can display literature books. Add ocean island details: seashells, starfish, crabs, etc. Students can go to the island for independent reading.

• Construct a semantic web with facts your students know about islands. Then ask them to list questions about islands they would like answered today.

Literary Exploration

The Cay by Theodore Taylor
Celia's Island Journal by Loretta Krupinski
The Greatest Treasure by Arcadio Lobato
Herbert's Treasure by Alice Low
If Once You Have Slept on an Island by Rachel Field
Island Rescue by Charles E. Martin
It's Mine! by Leo Lionni
The Kweeks of Kookatumdee by Bill Peet
The Little Island by Margaret Wise Brown
The Little Island by Golden MacDonald
L.L. Bear's Island Adventure by Kate Rowinski
Monroe's Island by Gregory Brooks
Muppet Treasure Island by Alison Inches
My Island Grandma by Kathryn Lasky
Puzzle Island by Paul Adshead
Robinson Crusoe by Daniel Defoe
Rotten Island by William Steig
This Island Isn't Big Enough for the Four of Us by Greer and Ruddiek
Treasure Island by Robert Louis Stevenson
Yanosh's Island by Yossi Abolafia

Treasure
Island

Treasure
Island

Treasure
Island

Language Experience

• Display a variety of everyday items and let students form cooperative groups to discuss how they would use each item to survive on a desert island.

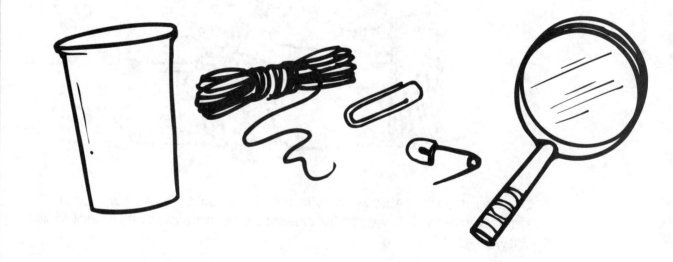

Writing Experience

- Provide each student with a glass bottle or baby food jar. Have them write rescue messages to put in the bottles or jars. Encourage them to decide what would be the most important thing to say in the limited amount of space to help identify their island and their need for rescue.

- Students can write, using these story starters:

  I would not like to live without . . .

  If I were stranded on a desert island, the thing I would miss most is . . .

  See reproducible on page 82.

Social Studies Experience

- Have students look in world atlases to locate familiar islands around the world.

Music/Dramatic Experience

- Let students role-play spending a day on a desert island. What would be fun? What would be hard?

Physical/Sensory Experience

- Play Musical Islands (a variation of Musical Chairs). Students pretend that each chair is an "island" as they are gradually eliminated one at a time.

Arts/Crafts Experience

- Let students work together to create a class mural of a desert island populated by shipwreck survivors.

- Let students make salt dough relief models of their own little islands. Bake at 350°F for an hour, then paint.

Salt Dough
1/2 cup flour
2/3 cup salt
1/3 cup water

Treasure Island
Treasure Island
Treasure Island

Extension Activities

- Anyone who is left alone on a desert island has to scrounge for whatever they can find to survive. Let students go on a mini scavenger hunt around the classroom or school for various items.

⚠ Serve tuna on crackers to represent "sea rations." Or students can eat foods that used to be eaten on ship voyages long ago (biscuits and honey, raisins, beef jerky).

Values Education Experience

- Encourage students to think about what they would miss most on a desert island. Are they grateful for those things or those people while they have them?

Follow-Up/Homework Idea

- Students can watch *The Muppets Treasure Island* movie or another "island" film with their families.

82

Rembrandt's Birthday

July 15

Setting the Stage
• Display copies of some of Rembrandt's paintings around related literature.

Historical Background
Dutch painter Rembrandt was born on this day in 1606 in Holland. He died in 1669.

1606

Literary Exploration

Introducing Rembrandt by Alexander Sturgis
Rembrandt by Ernest Lloyd Raboff
Rembrandt by Gary Schwartz
Rembrandt by Mike Venezia
Rembrandt Takes a Walk by Mark Strand
A Weekend with Rembrandt by Pascal Bonafoux

Language Experience

- How many new words can your students make using the letters in *Rembrandt?*

Social Studies Experience

- Study the life and artistic contributions of Rembrandt.

- Have students locate Holland on a world map. What continent is it part of?

Music/Dramatic Experience

- Let students experiment with oil painting as they listen to music representative of the 17th century. Have them wear aprons or old shirts to cover their clothes as they paint.

Arts/Crafts Experience

- Rembrandt was known for his ability to contrast light and dark in his oil paintings as well as his way of capturing people's realistic facial expressions. Let your students try using these art techniques as they paint pictures.

- Have students choose partners, then take turns painting or drawing one another's portraits.

Rembrandt

Extension Activities

- Take your class on a field trip to a nearby museum that exhibits oil paintings. Can they find Rembrandt's work?

Rembrandt

Follow-Up/Homework Idea

- Students can check to see how many watercolor or oil paintings they have in their homes.

Rembrandt

Kisses
and Hugs

Kisses
and Hugs

Kisses
and Hugs

Kisses and Hugs Day

July 16

Setting the Stage

• Display a giant Hershey's Kiss™ around related literature to gather excitement about today's activities.

Historical Background

Kissing was prohibited in England on this day in 1439 in an effort to prevent the spread of diseases! It must not have worked because the rule was soon changed and kissing became legal again.

Literary Exploration

A Book of Hugs by Dave Ross
Catch Me & Kiss Me and Say It Again by Clyde Watson
How Many Kisses Goodnight? by Jean Monrad
Hug Me by Patti Stren
Hugs by Alice McLerran
Hugs and Kisses by Winthrop
It's Your First Kiss, Charlie Brown by Charles M. Schulz
A Kiss for Little Bear by Else Holmelund Minarik
Kiss Is Round by Blossom Budney
Kisses by Alice McLerran
Kisses from Rosa by Petra Mathers
Octopus Hug by Laurence Pringle
Sloppy Kisses by Elizabeth Winthrop
Throw a Kiss, Harry by Mary Eileen Chalmers
Willie's Not the Hugging Kind by Joyce Barrett

Language Experience

• Create a Venn diagram depicting the similarities and differences between kisses and hugs.

• Let students brainstorm as many words as they can that rhyme with the words *kiss* and *hug*.

Writing Experience

• Let students write about whether they like a hug or kiss the best and why. See reproducible on page 89.

• Challenge students to write about the differences in hugs and kisses from Mom, from Grandpa, from a friend and from a pet!

Arts/Crafts Experience

- Let students draw pictures of those they like to show affection to (such as members of the family).

Extension Activities

⚠ Let students make Rice Crispy™ treats in the shape of giant kisses (using plastic funnels).

⚠ Serve foil-covered Kisses™ and Hugs™ candies for a special treat.

Follow-Up/Homework Idea

- Encourage students to go home and give their family members big hugs and kisses!

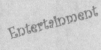

Entertainment Day

July 17

Setting the Stage
• Display a spotlight and a microphone around related literature to get students excited about the day's emphasis.

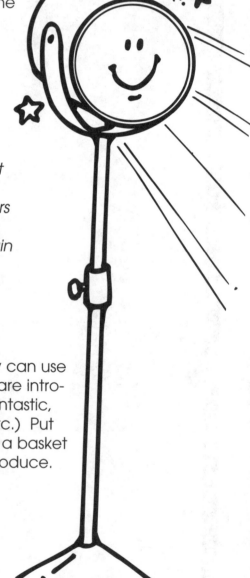

Literary Exploration
Eddycat and Buddy Entertain a Guest by Ada Barnett
Entertainment: Screen, Stage and Stars by Jacqueline Morley
Nothing's Impossible! Stunts To Entertain by Jeff Sheridan

Language Experience
• Let student think of superlatives they can use to introduce one another as if they are introducing famous stars. (Examples: fantastic, amazing, hilarious, multi-talented, etc.) Put students' names on slips of paper in a basket and let them draw who they will introduce.

90

Writing Experience

• Actors, musicians and other professional entertainers have agents who represent them especially to the press. Challenge each student to write a "press release" about himself or herself, describing a talent or ability. Tell them this is not a time to be humble, but to brag a little, making themselves look good since it's just for fun.

• Let students write about their favorite entertainers and explain why they like them so much.

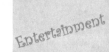

Math Experience

• Let students use star stickers as math manipulatives today. Present them with problems and let them stick stars on paper to indicate their answers.

Social Studies Experience

• Create a class time line of famous entertainment figures throughout history.

• Let students do additional research about favorite entertainers and share the information with the rest of the class.

Music/Dramatic Experience

• Let students perform a music video (by taping them on a camcorder) as they perform their favorite hits.

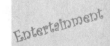

Arts/Crafts Experience

• Let students design their own costumes for the class talent show (see below). Provide craft materials as well as some "dress up" clothing for them to use.

• Students can create posters advertising the talent show, explaining what the entertainment will be, while others make tickets to hand out for the show.

• Let students each draw a picture and write a description of a favorite entertainer. They can compile the pages in a class book called *Entertaining Entertainers*. When the book is completed, keep it on a bookshelf for students to look through when they have extra time.

Extension Activities

• Encourage students to contribute in some way to a class talent show presented to another class.

⚠ Some students can make a snack to serve after the show (popcorn or crackers and cheese with fruit).

Follow-Up/Homework Idea

• Students can display their talents to entertain their families. Encourage them to ask their family members to be a part of the entertainment, too!

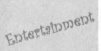

Tennis, Anyone? Day

July 18

Setting the Stage

- Display a tennis ball and racket alongside related literature to gather interest in today's activities.

Historical Background

Tennis was introduced in the United States in 1874. Since then it has become one of America's favorite sports.

Literary Exploration

I Want to Be a Tennis Player by Eugene Baker
Jenny and the Tennis Nut by Janet Schulman
Tennis by Donna Bailey
Tennis for Boys and Girls by George Sullivan
What Is a Tennis? by Anthony Ravielli

Math Experience

- Let students take turns seeing how many times they can bounce a tennis ball without a break. Let the class count for them as they bounce the ball. Keep track of their scores on the board.

Science/Health Experience
• Review safety while playing tennis.

Social Studies Experience
• Learn about tennis greats such as Billie Jean King, Arthur Ashe, Andre Agassi, Tracy Austin, Jennifer Capriati and others.

• Find out where the major tennis tournaments are played and have students locate the places on a world map. (Example: Wimbledon—London, England)

Physical/Sensory Experience
• Let students play this relay game between two teams. Each player tries to hold a tennis ball between his or her knees while moving quickly to a designated area and back.

• Teach students the basics of tennis. Take them outside to the tennis courts to practice hitting the ball over the net.

94

Tennis, Anyone?

Arts/Crafts Experience

• Let students sculpt tennis players from clay or aluminum foil.

• Students can make their own tennis rackets from cardboard and string, then try hitting Nerf™ balls or crumpled up paper balls.

Extension Activities

• Invite a local high school tennis player to come and talk to your students about the game of tennis.

⚠ Check out a tennis video from your local library for students to watch. As they watch they can snack on popcorn "balls."

Cow-Wow! Day

July 19

Setting the Stage

- Display pictures of cows, and ceramic or toy cows around related literature. Greet your students wearing a milk "moustache" for fun!

- Create a bulletin board displaying student work alongside a picture of a cow with the caption: "We're MOO'ving Along in Our School Work!"

- Construct a semantic web with facts your students know (or want to know) about cows to help you structure your day.

Literary Exploration

Calico Cows by Arlene Dubanevich
The Chocolate Cow by Lilian Obligado
Cows in the Parlor: A Visit to the Dairy Farm by Cynthia McFarland
The Cow That Went Oink by Bernard Most
The Cow Who Could Tap Dance by Teddy Slater
The Cow Who Wouldn't Come Down by Paul Brett Johnson
From Cow to Shoe by Ali Mitgutsch
George Washington's Cows by David Small
Green Grass and White Milk by Aliki
Hana, the No-Cow Wife by Pat Bagley
Henry and the Cow Problem by Iona Whishaw
How Now, Brown Cow? by Alice Schertle
Hunting the White Cow by Tres Seymour
I Want to Be a Dairy Farmer by Carla Greene
Last Cow on the White House Lawn by Barbara Seuling
Milk Rock by Jeff Kaufman
Moo Moo, Brown Cow by Jakki Wood
Morning Milking by Linda Morris
Ms. Blanche, the Spotless Cow by Zidrou
No Moon, No Milk by Chris Babcock
"Not Now!" Said the Cow by Joanne Oppenheim
An Occasional Cow by Polly Horvath
One Cow Moo Moo! by David Bennett
Out to Pasture! Jokes About Cows by Joanne Bernstein
The Silver Cow by Susan Coop
The Smallest Cow in the World by Katherine Paterson
Supermoo! by Babette Cole
There's a Cow in the Road by Reeve Lindbergh
Tiny, Tiny Boy and the Big, Big Cow by Nancy Van Laan
What a Wonderful Day to Be a Cow by Carolyn Lesser

Language Experience

• Let students brainstorm other words that have the "ow" sound as in *cow*.

• Let students have some fun with cow talk. They can imagine how cows, if they could talk, would say certain words. (Examples: marvellous = moo-arvelous, morning = moo-orning, move = moove)

Science/Health Experience

- Learn about cows and their habitat. Discuss how cows benefit us in our daily lives (milk, cheese, hamburger, leather, etc.).

- Study the process milk goes through from the cow to the jug in the refrigerator.

Social Studies Experience

- Have students look in an atlas to find cattle grazing areas or dairy farming in the United States. What state is famous for its dairy products?

Music/Dramatic Experience

- Let students do stand-up comedy routines, telling jokes from the book *Out to Pasture! Jokes About Cows* written by Joanne Bernstein.

- Teach your students the song "The Clever Cow" by Janeen Brady.

98

Physical/Sensory Experience

- Students will get a kick out of this sensory experience! Punch pinholes in each finger of a surgical rubber glove. Then fill it with milk, leaving space at the top for gathering. Let students try their hand at "milking" while an adult holds the glove gathered at the top over a bucket. Ask students to tell what milking felt like.

Arts/Crafts Experience

- Students can make cow puppets with paper bags and felt or construction paper cutouts of cow head patterns. See patterns on page 101.

- Let fast finishers work together on a class mural of cows in a pasture.

- Students can design dioramas of cow scenes making small clay or cardboard cows to stand in them.

Cow-Wow!

Cow-Wow!

Cow-Wow!

Extension Activities

⚠ Serve "Mud" Pie (chocolate pie) and Purple Cow Milk Shakes! To make the milk shakes, put a scoop of ice cream in a cup or glass of grape juice. For a frostier milk shake, add ice cream to frozen grape juice concentrate and mix it in a blender for a moment or two. Serve right away.

⚠ Provide a variety of vegetables (celery, carrots, radishes, raw broccoli, etc.) for students to graze on as cows do.

• Invite a dairy farmer to visit your class or take students on a field trip to a dairy farm. They might even get a chance to milk a real cow!

Follow-Up/Homework Idea

• Encourage students to drink all their milk at dinnertime!

Cow-Wow!

100

Man on the Moon Day

July 20

Setting the Stage

• Display pictures of the moon around related literature to get students excited about the day.

• Construct a semantic web with facts your students know about the moon. List questions they would like to have answered today.

Historical Background

On this day in 1969, Neil A. Armstrong was the first man to walk on the moon.

102

Literary Exploration

Blue Moon Soup Spoon by Mimi Otey
A Bucketful of Moon by Toby Talbot
To Catch the Moon by Dinie Akkerman
A Close Look at the Moon by G. Jeffrey Taylor
Elephant Moon by Bijou LeTord
Going to the Moon by James Muirden
Lemon Moon by Kay Chorao
Many Moons by James Thurber
The Mice on the Moon by Rodney Peppe
Moon Bear by Frank Asch
Mooncake by Frank Asch
Moon Dragon by Frances Manushkin
Moongame by Frank Asch
Moon, Stars, Frogs and Friends by Patricia MacLachlan
The Moon Was the Best by Charlotte Zolotow
Munia and the Moon by Asun Balzola
Owl Moon by Jane Yolen
Papa, Please Get the Moon for Me by Eric Carle
The Princess and the Moon by Daisaku Ikeda
Rabbit Mooncakes by Hoong Yee Lee Krakauer
Sing Down the Moon by Scott O'Dell
Through Moon and Stars and Night Skies by Ann Warren Turner
What the Moon Saw by Brian Wildsmith
While the Moon Shines Bright by Jeanne Whitehouse Peterson

Language Experience

• Let students brainstorm other words that have the "oo" sound has in *moon*.

Writing Experience

• Let students visualize themselves in Neil Armstrong's place, stepping onto the moon for the first time. Ask them to write about how they might feel. See reproducible on page 107.

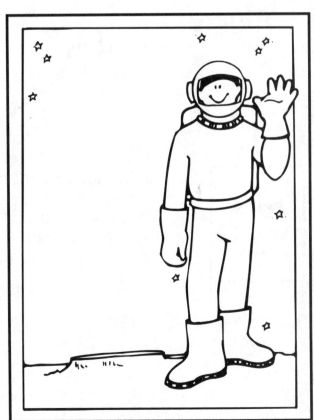

103

Math Experience

- Lead students in a study of the phases of the moon during the next month, coordinating it with a review of reading the calendar.

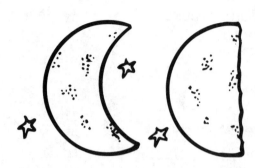
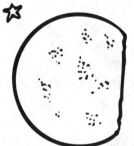

Man on the Moon

Science/Health Experience

- Begin a science unit on the moon.

Man on the Moon

Social Studies Experience

- Learn about the history of Apollo space flights. Let students work on a time line noting historical flights.

Man on the Moon

104

TLC10485 Copyright © Teaching & Learning Company, Carthage, IL 62321-0010

Music/Dramatic Experience

• Sing "Sally Go Round the Sun."

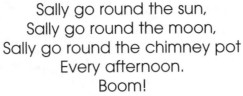

Sally go round the sun,
Sally go round the moon,
Sally go round the chimney pot
Every afternoon.
Boom!
(On the word *Boom*, students all fall down.)

Physical/Sensory Experience

• Let students simulate the movements of the Earth, moon and sun.
Divide the class into groups so each person gets a chance to act out
a specific part. Each group should have students to be the Earth, the
moon and the sun. Have the Earth rotate (spin on its axis) and
revolve around the sun counterclockwise as directed, rotating west to
east. The moon revolves around the Earth counterclockwise. The sun
stands still.

Man on
the Moon

Man on
the Moon

Man on
the Moon

Man on
the Moon

Man on
the Moon

Man on
the Moon

Arts/Crafts Experience

- Let students sponge gray and white paint onto a paper plate cut in the shape of a moon or left as a full moon. It can be glued onto a background finger-painted like a blue sky. Foil-shaped stars can be added for detail.

Extension Activities

- Invite an astronomer to come and talk to your class about the moon.

Values Education Experience

- The expression "reach for the moon" means to try something that seems impossible. Ask students to share times when they have tried hard to do a difficult task or learn something new. Talk about persistence.

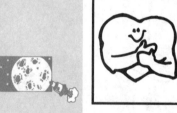

Follow-Up/Homework Idea

- Encourage students to get permission to lie outside tonight and observe the shape of the moon (half, full, crescent).

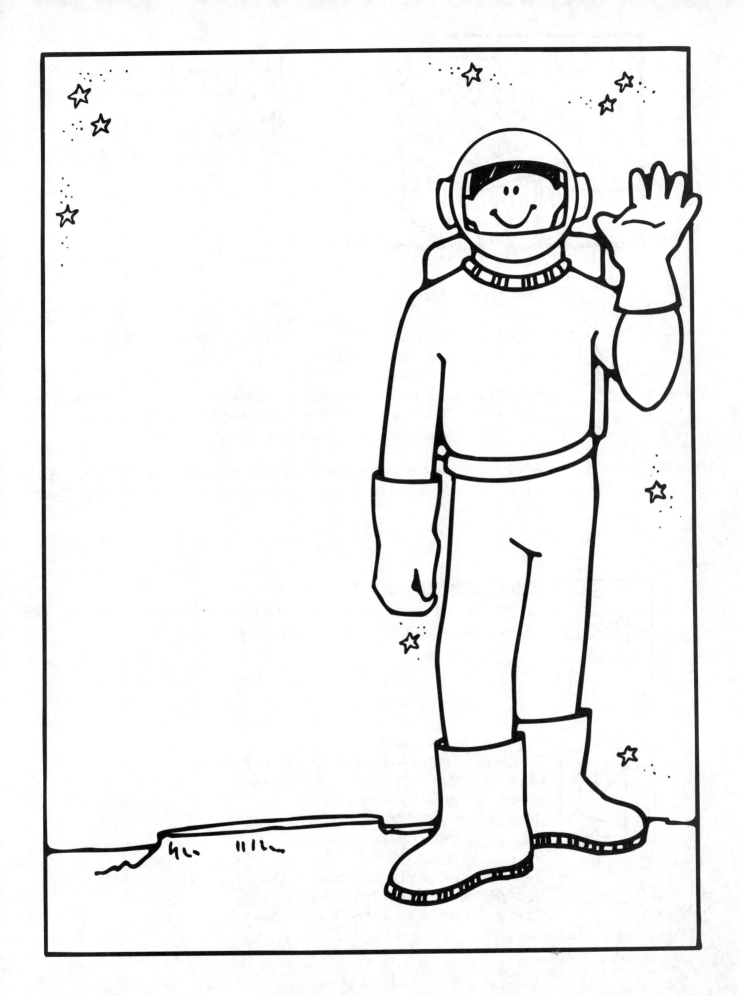

Blueberry
Bash

Blueberry
Bash

Blueberry
Bash

Blueberry Bash Day

July 21

Setting the Stage

• Cut large circles from various shades of blue construction paper and scatter them all over the room—on the walls, floor, desks, etc. Let students tape blue circles on their clothes, too.

• Invite students to wear blue clothing today in honor of the blueberry. Greet them at the classroom door with a bowl of fresh blueberries. Let them take a few for a tasty way to start the day.

• Display blueberry related books on a table around a bowl of blueberries. Above the table mount the caption: "A Book Is a Berry Good Treat!"

Historical Background

July is National Blueberries Month, a time to make people aware that it's the peak month for the delicious, good-for-you fruit.

Literary Exploration

Blueberries for the Queen by Katherine Paterson
Blueberries for Sal by Robert McCloskey
Blueberry Mouse by Alice Low
The Blueberry Pie Elf by Jane Thayer
Blueberry Shoe by Ann Dixon
The Blueberry Train by C.L.G. Martin and Angela Trotta
The Bobbsey Twins on Blueberry Island by Laura Lee Hope
Dear Mr. Blueberry by Simon James
Peter in Blueberry Land by Elsa Beskow

Language Experience

- Point out to students that when they want to make the word *blueberry* plural, they drop the "y" and add "ies." Have them brainstorm other words they need to do this to in order to make them plural. Write the singular and plural forms of the words they suggest.

- Challenge students to think of adjectives that begin with "b" to describe or connect with "blueberry" or "blueberries" for a TV commercial. (beautiful, big, blast)

- Point out that the name of today's celebration is Blueberry Bash Day. Ask students to define the word *bash*, then suggest synonyms for it.

Writing Experience

- Have each student write a short adventure story about meeting a bear while picking blueberries.

- Let students use the following story starters for some fun writing experience:

    Everyone was surprised at the person who won the blueberry pie eating contest . . .

    Blueberry pie used to be my favorite dessert, but not anymore!

    My friend and I picked blueberries all morning, but I noticed that he ate as many as he put in his pail. Suddenly, I noticed that his face was a funny blue color . . .

Blueberry Bash

Math Experience

- Let students use blueberries as math manipulatives to review counting by twos, threes, fives and tens.

- Give each student two blue circles. Have them write a math problem on one circle and the answer on the other circle. Then collect the circles and put them in two piles—a problem pile and an answer pile. Let students take turns choosing problem "berries" from the one pile, then finding the answers in the other pile.

- Have students measure items in your classroom in "blueberry size." They line up blueberries along the length and width of each item, then count the blueberries and write down the dimensions of the item.

Blueberry Bash

TLC10485 Copyright © Teaching & Learning Company, Carthage, IL 62321-0010

109

Science/Health Experience

• Blueberries are considered to be a "power food" because they have high antioxidant capacities. Have students research what antioxidants are and how they affect people's health. They can report their findings to the rest of the class.

• Study how and where blueberries grow. In what kind of climate do they grow best?

Social Studies Experience

• Bears love blueberries. Studies have shown that they will go 10 to 15 miles to sniff out a blueberry patch. Study other animals that love blueberries.

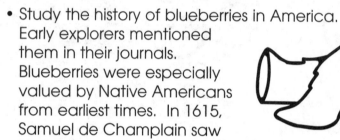

• Study the history of blueberries in America. Early explorers mentioned them in their journals. Blueberries were especially valued by Native Americans from earliest times. In 1615, Samuel de Champlain saw Native Americans harvesting wild blueberries near Lake Huron. Lewis and Clark ate blueberries served to them by Native Americans on their expedition.

Music/Dramatic Experience

• Let students work in pairs or small groups to write raps or songs about blueberries to familiar tunes. Help them get started by brainstorming rhyming words (blue, new, too, you, few, grew; berry, merry, fairy, dairy, scary; eat, treat, neat, beat; delight, right, bite, might, etc.). When they're done, let them perform their raps or songs for the rest of the class.

• Let students work together to write a skit about some children, a bear cub and a blueberry bush. Then let the students choose class members to act out their skit.

Physical/Sensory Experience

• Place the following items in a paper sack: blueberries, buttons, round pebbles, small round candies, peanuts and other items that resemble the feel of blueberries. Let students take turns reaching a hand into the sack and feeling for the blueberries. The only rules are that they must not squeeze the items and they only have 15 seconds to find a blueberry. Warn them that squeezing the blueberries will turn their fingers blue, so when they take their hand out of the sack, everyone will know they broke the rules and they will be disqualified. (If a blueberry is smashed during the game, transfer the items to a clean sack.)

Arts/Crafts Experience

- Let students paint pictures using only shades of blue. Have them wear aprons or old shirts over their clothes to keep them clean.

- Hand out toothpicks and blueberries. Let students try making blueberry people by connecting the berries with the toothpicks. Have them wear aprons or old shirts to protect their clothes and to keep their hands from getting stained, have them wear clear, plastic gloves.

- Students can create advertisements encouraging people to eat blueberries. Encourage them to be creative and also include all the good things they've learned about blueberries.

- Provide primary colors of tempera paints and plastic bowls. Let students mix paint colors to try and come up with the exact color of blueberries. Let them vote on which color is closest to fresh berries.

Extension Activities

- If someone in your area grows blueberries, get permission to take your students there on a field trip. Maybe they can even pick some!

- Invite a local blueberry grower to visit your class and answer their questions about blueberries.

- Invite a local baker or chef to come and talk to your students about some delicious ways to use blueberries in cooking.

⚠ Let students each bring fruit to make class fruit salad: blueberries, strawberries, kiwi, bananas, mangoes, pineapples, apples, pears, peaches, plums, oranges, etc. You may want to assign each student what fruit to bring so there'll be plenty of variety. Put a huge bowl in the middle of a table. Let each student put his or her fruit in the bowl. Provide knives (not very sharp) for older students to cut up their fruit. You'll need to do the cutting for younger students. When all the fruit is in the bowl, mix it together, then serve it in plastic bowls to the class. For an extra special treat, put a dip of vanilla ice cream in the center of each bowl of fruit. Have enough plastic spoons and napkins to go around.

⚠ Is one of your students' parents known for his or her baking? Ask that person to bake a blueberry pie for your class. Serve it with vanilla ice cream for a great way to end today's celebration.

Blueberry Bash

Blueberry Bash

Blueberry Bash

Follow-Up/Homework Idea

⚠ Encourage students to ask permission from their parents to help them make blueberry muffins for a family treat.

Yummy Blueberry Muffins (for a dozen muffins)

Ingredients
1 1/2 cups flour
1/2 cup granulated sugar
1 tablespoon baking powder
1/2 teaspoon salt
1 egg
1/2 cup milk
1/4 cup melted margarine
1 cup blueberries

Directions
1. Sift the flour into a bowl.
2. Add the sugar, baking powder and salt and mix together.
3. In another bowl, beat the egg slightly with the milk.
4. Stir the egg and milk mixture into the dry ingredients.
5. Stir the margarine into the mix until the ingredients are blended.
6. Lightly fold in the blueberries.
7. Fill greased muffin cups about 2/3 full with the batter.
8. Bake the muffins in a 400°F oven for 20-25 minutes.
9. Be sure to eat them while they're warm!

• If students aren't able to make blueberry muffins, they can ask their parents to make pancakes from a boxed mix and throw in some blueberries!

Blueberry
Bash

Blueberry
Bash

Blueberry
Bash

Statue of Liberty Day

July 22

Setting the Stage

• Greet your students dressed as the "Lady of the Lamp!" Drape a sheet over your shoulder. You can spray gold paint over the sheet and make a crown of aluminum foil-covered sugar cones glued to a Styrofoam™ ring. Cover a flashlight with a fringe of red tissue paper. Hold it in your raised right hand and speak with a French accent.

• Display pictures of the Statue of Liberty surrounded by related literature.

• Construct a semantic web with facts your students know about the Statue of Liberty. List questions they want answered today.

Historical Background

Emma Lazarus, the poet who wrote the words engraved on the Statue of Liberty, was born on this day in 1849. The Statue of Liberty was a gift to the United States from France. It was shipped to New York City in 1885, assembled and dedicated in 1886.

Literary Exploration

Emma Lazarus by Diane Lefer
Emma Lazarus by Natalie Miller
How the Second Grade Got $8205.50 to Visit the Statue of Liberty
   by Nathan Zimelman
I Lift My Lamp: Emma Lazarus and the Statue of Liberty
   by Nancy Smiler Levinson
The Littles Visit the Statue of Liberty by Lorentz Carlson
The Statue of Liberty by Natalie Miller
The Statue of Liberty by Lucille Recht Penner
The Statue of Liberty by William Shapiro
The Story of the Statue of Liberty by Betsy Maestro

Language Experience

• How many new words can your students make using the letters in *Statue of Liberty*.

Writing Experience

• Ask students to imagine that the Statue of Liberty can talk. Have them write about what she might say. See reproducible on page 117.

• Let students imagine they are immigrants coming to America from lands where they had little freedom. They can write what their thoughts are when they see the Statue of Liberty.

114

Math Experience

• Measure on your playground the Statue of Liberty's size (height—151 feet, nose—4 1/2 feet, eyes—2 1/2 feet, mouth—3 feet, fingernail—13 inches, length of torch—21 feet).

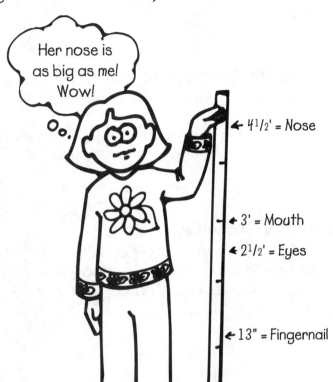

Her nose is as big as *me!* Wow!

← 4 1/2' = Nose

← 3' = Mouth

← 2 1/2' = Eyes

← 13" = Fingernail

Social Studies Experience

• Study the history surrounding the Statue of Liberty.

• Let students research biographical information about Emma Lazarus to share with the rest of the class.

Music/Dramatic Experience

• Let students audition to be the "voice" of the Statue of Liberty. Let them read Lazarus' poem with feeling. Play patriotic music in the background.

Statue of
Liberty

Statue of
Liberty

Statue of
Liberty

Physical/Sensory Experience

• Play Emma, Emma, Lazarus, a new version of Duck, Duck, Goose. Students say Emma Lazarus' name as they tap students gently with a rolled up paper "torch," then race around the circle to get back in place.

Arts/Crafts Experience

• The Statue of Liberty is a symbol to all the world of America's democracy and freedom, a beacon of new opportunity. Let students use clay to sculpt their own symbols of freedom.

Extension Activities

• Serve "torch" ice cream cones! Top sugar cones with rainbow sherbet and insert a paper flame for a fun Statue of Liberty treat!

Values Education Experience

• Today is a good day to discuss liberty. What is it? How do we show that we value it? Why do we have it when some other countries do not?

Follow-Up/Homework Idea

• Encourage students to be the kind of people Emma Lazarus envisioned Americans to be (kind, welcoming and friendly) whenever they are.

Shooting Stars Day

July 23

Setting the Stage

- Display pictures of common constellations (Ursa Major—Great Bear, Ursa Minor—Little Bear, Cygnus—Swan) on a bulletin board. Let students decorate their own imaginary constellations by drawing figures with white chalk on black construction paper and adding silver or gold stickers to represent stars. Display their constellations on the board.

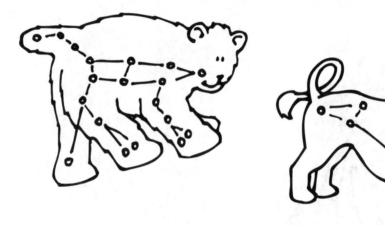

- Display pictures of stars or clusters of stars in constellations around related literature.

- Construct a semantic web with facts your students know (or want to know) about stars to help you structure the day.

Historical Background

Astrological signs such as Pisces are constellations in the sky. Today marks the day that the zodiac sign, Leo the Lion, begins.

Literary Exploration

After Dark by Blossom Budney
All About Stars by Lawrence Jeffries
The Big Dipper by Franklyn M. Branley
The Bird and the Stars by Paul Showers
Close Your Eyes by Jean Marzollo
Do You Know About the Stars? by Mae Blacker Freeman
Find the Constellations by H.A. Rey
Knock at a Star by X.J. Kennedy
Peterkin Meets a Star by Emilie Boon
Stargazers by Gail Gibbons
The Star Grazers by Christine Widman
Stars by Melvin Berger
The Stars: A New Way to See Them by H. A. Rey
The Stars Tonight by John Polgreen
The Sun, Our Nearest Star by Franklyn M. Branley

Language Experience

• Brainstorm as a class words that contain *star* (*starfish, start, starship*).

Writing Experience

• Let students write what they would wish for if they wished on a star. See reproducible on page 124.

• Students can use these story starters to write science fiction tales:

    I saw a falling star land just down the street . . .

    As I stood looking up at the night sky, the stars began whirling around . . .

If I wished upon a star...

Math Experience

- Hand out gummed stars for students to use as manipulatives for counting, adding and subtracting.

- Have students write a number on a star shape. Then call on two of them to hold up their stars. See who in the class can pop up first with the sum of the star numbers. Or have them multiply the numbers. Keep the action going for several minutes.

Science/Health Experience

- Begin a science unit on stars. Students are used to seeing images of pointed stars. They may not understand that a star is a huge ball of gases, such as our huge star, the sun. Of course, the sun is much closer than the other stars.

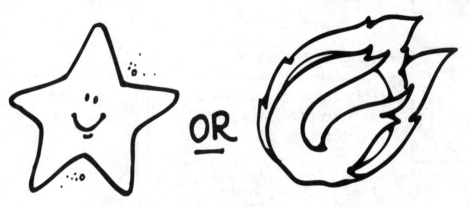

- Let students grow grass seed stars. They cut sponges in star shapes, then plant grass seed in them. If they keep their sponges moist and in direct sunlight, they'll soon have grass!

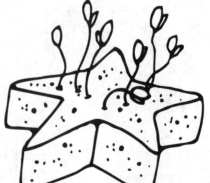

120

Social Studies Experience

- Study the history of stargazing. Explain that early navigators such as Columbus often charted their courses based on the stars and their constellations.

Music/Dramatic Experience

- Younger students can sing "Twinkle, Twinkle, Little Star." Let older students make up new words to the old tune.

Twinkle, Twinkle, Little Star!

Arts/Crafts Experience

- Provide students with black and white construction paper. They draw an outline of a constellation on the black sheet with chalk. Then they poke holes where the stars are and erase the chalk marks. When they place the white paper behind the black paper, they'll have a constellation picture.

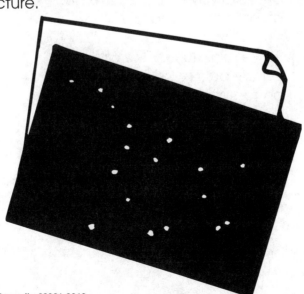

Arts/Crafts Experience continued

- Each student can draw an outline of a star constellation on dark paper, then glue miniature marshmallows on the stars or decorate them with a silver marker.

- Students can make stargazing dioramas out of shoe boxes with a peephole cut in one end. They can cut stars in the lid to shed a little light, then decorate the inside with construction paper or tissue paper constellations.

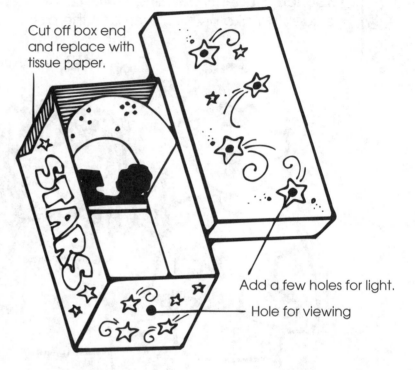

Cut off box end and replace with tissue paper.

Add a few holes for light.

Hole for viewing

Extension Activities

- Visit a nearby planetarium for a class field trip.

⚠ Students can try to make their own stars by biting off the corners of large marshmallows.

⚠ Serve miniature Milky Way™ candy bars or chunks of cheese on toothpicks for a treat!

Values Education Experience

• Reinforce that each person in your classroom is a star! Prepare an ongoing bulletin board with the caption: "Our STAR _____ (fill in name)!" Students can take turns being the star of the classroom with their pictures and work samples displayed. Give them special opportunities in the classroom during this time also. Express your love and affection for them individually. Let them know they are valued as part of your classroom team! See pattern on page 125.

Follow-Up/Homework Idea

• Encourage students to do some stargazing tonight with their families. They can look for the Big Dipper or maybe they'll see a shooting star!

STAR
Our

Pioneer Day
July 24

Setting the Stage

- Display pictures of pioneers crossing the American plains around related literature.

Historical Background

Brigham Young and other pioneers reached Salt Lake Valley on this day in 1847 after a long, arduous journey across the plains. Many other Americans traveled by wagon across the country to settle in the western frontier. They battled Indian attacks, disease and dangerous routes across mountains and raging rivers to make their dreams come true.

Literary Exploration

An American Pioneer Family by Robin May
Iva Dunnit and the Big Wind by Carol Purdy
My Great Grandmother, the Pioneer Woman by Lynn M. LaGrange
Pioneer Art in America by Carolyn Bailey
Pioneer Bear by Joan Sandin
Pioneers by Robert Miller

Language Experience

• How many words can your students think of that rhyme with *pioneer*? (deer, fear, steer, appear)

Writing Experience

• Let students imagine they are pioneers crossing the plains to new homes, seeking new opportunities. Have them write journal entries about their experiences and feelings.

Math Experience

• Let your students measure the dimensions of a typical prairie schooner (covered wagon) on the school playground. To help them get a feel for how small the wagon's space was for storing everything the pioneers owned, have students sit together in the measured off area. A typical schooner was 4 feet wide by 12 feet long.

Social Studies Experience

• Learn about the history of pioneers moving west and the challenges they faced.

• Discuss changes from pioneer days to present times: differences in travel, homes, conveniences, work tools, entertainment, etc.

Music/Dramatic Experience

• Check out some pioneer/western music from a local library to add a little pioneer flavor while students are working on their projects.

• Sing some songs with a pioneer flavor: "Sweet Betsy from Pike," "Home on the Range," "She'll Be Coming 'Round the Mountain."

Physical/Sensory Experience

• Teach students basic square dancing steps, a favorite pioneer pastime. Play some music and have a hoedown!

• Host an old-fashioned ball and jacks tournament! Or let students play marbles.

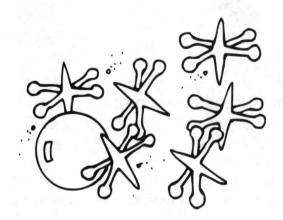

128

Arts/Crafts Experience

- Let students try art projects from *Pioneer Art in America*, written by Carolyn Bailey.

- Let students work together to make a prairie scene with tall grass and flowers. Use toy figures of people, animals and wagons to make it come alive.

Extension Activities

⚠ Make and serve Ginger Cookies, a favorite pioneer treat.

Ginger Cookies

1/2 c. sugar
1/2 c. molasses
1/3 c. shortening
1/3 c. water
Mix together then add:
1 egg
Mix in another bowl:
3 1/2 c. flour
1/2 t. bakingsoda
1/2 t. cinnamon
1/2 t. ginger
1/4 t. salt

Gradually add dry ingredients to the former. Shape mixture into balls and place them on a greased cookie sheet. Bake at 350° F for 8-10 minutes.

Pioneer Day

Pioneer Day

Follow-Up/Homework Idea

⚠ Serve a typical pioneer meal of beef jerky, fried potatoes, corn bread and honey.

Pioneer Day

Beat the Heat Day

July 25

Beat the
Heat

Setting the Stage
- Cut a huge sun from shiny yellow paper and mount it at the center of a bulletin board covered with blue paper. Have students bring summer photos of themselves with their families (swimming, mowing the grass, working in the garden, picnicking, riding bikes and doing other summer activities).

- Display covers of books that would be fun reading for students with the caption: "Beat the Heat with a Cool Book!"

Beat the
Heat

Historical Background
High summer, July 3 through August 15 are the hottest days of the year in the Northern Hemisphere. They are called the "dog days" of summer.

Literary Exploration
Betsy and Tacy Go over the Big Hill by Maud Hart Lovelace
Caterpillar Spring, Butterfly Summer by Susan Hood
Hot Dog by Molly Coxe
Muddles, Puddles & Sunshine by Winston's Wish
Stage Fright on a Summer Night by Mary Pope Osborne
Strawberry Girl by Lois Lenski
Summer of the Sea Serpent by Pope Osborne
Thimble Summer by Elizabeth Enright

Beat the
Heat

Language Experience

- Create a listening center in a corner of the room with headphones, cassette or CD player, and books on tape or CD. Encourage students to take advantage of the center whenever they finish their work and have extra time.

- Suspend a clothesline across a corner of the room that can be used for announcements and special features. For today, cut articles of clothing from colored paper and hang them with tiny clothespins on the line. On each piece of clothing, write a book genre your students might enjoy reading to encourage them to vary their reading this summer.

Writing Experience

- Challenge students to write about the hottest day they can remember. What happened? If they can't remember a particularly hot day, they can make one up!

- Students will enjoy writing about unusual ways to cool off on a hot day. Encourage them to use their imagination to come up with ideas no one has thought of before.

- Let students write rhyming poems about hot summer days, using adjectives that make the reader really feel the heat. You may want to let them brainstorm rhyming words they can use in their poems. List them on the board as they suggest them (heat, beat, feet, treat; hot, lot, not, spot, etc.). They can write their poems on yellow paper sun circles. Display the poems on a bulletin board or a hallway for everyone to read.

Math Experience

• Let students compare temperatures day by day, figuring out how many degrees they change. Have them compare today's temperature with the temperature six months ago.

• Let students survey one another about their favorite hot weather activities. They can show the information on a class bar graph.

• Give students play money, the same amount for everyone. Print some summertime "expenses" on the board (ice cream cone—$.75, root beer—$.65, swimming at the pool—$1.50, movie—$3.50, etc.). Let students decide what they want to spend their money on, then figure out if they have enough money for what they want.

Beat the Heat

Science/Health Experience

• Study ice—how long it takes water to freeze at particular temperatures, how quickly it melts back to a liquid in hot temperatures, how it cools drinks, etc.

• Let students research to find out how "the dog days of summer" got their name. They can report their findings to the rest of the class.

• Study the dangers of staying in the sun too long without protection such as a hat and sunscreen. Find out the symptoms of sunstroke. Discuss how students should take care of their health in the hot summertime.

• Talk about how to care for pets to keep them safe and healthy in the summertime (make sure they have fresh water, provide shelter from the sun, don't leave them inside closed cars, etc.).

• Let students research to compare average temperatures in your area over the last 10 or 20 years. Is there a clear indication that summers are getting hotter or cooler? That winters are getting milder or more severe? Ask students to express their opinions about global warming.

• The sun is hot enough where we are in the summer, but how hot is it on the sun's surface? Students can research to find out. Discuss how hot the Earth would be if we were a little closer to the sun or how cold it would be if we were just a little farther away from it.

• Let students research where the hottest temperatures occur in the United States.

Beat the Heat

Beat the Heat

TLC10485 Copyright © Teaching & Learning Company, Carthage, IL 62321-0010

Social Studies Experience

- Have students locate the consistently hottest locations in the United States.

- Study how people have tried to "beat the heat" over the years from bringing snow down from the mountains to cool Emperor Nero's drinks to ice boxes to modern air conditioning. Students may find some of the lengths people went to rather humorous.

- Students will enjoy learning about the kinds of animals that inhabit the hottest parts of the world, such as the desert or the tropical jungles. How do those animals survive when they are taken from their habitat and brought to zoos in this country where the temperatures are cooler?

Physical/Sensory Experience

- Take students outside in the warm sunshine. Ask them to describe how the sun feels on their bare skin. Have them touch the sidewalk. Is it hot? Have them touch the grass. Is it hot? Have them touch a variety of other items (metal, brick or stone, soil, leaves). Ask them which items reflect the heat of the sun the most.

△ Serve ice cream or iced lemonade. Have students eat or drink slowly. Can they feel the cool treat going down? How long does it take before they start to feel cooler?

Beat the
Heat

Beat the
Heat

Beat the
Heat

Arts/Crafts Experience

- If it's a nice summer day, get permission to take students outside and let them draw summer pictures on the sidewalk.

- Let students paint pictures of where they like to go on summer vacation. Provide paints, paintbrushes, art paper and aprons or old shirts to protect their clothing. You may want to talk about some of their favorite vacation spots before they begin painting to help them decide what they want to picture (mountains, beach, amusement park, lake, zoo, etc.). After their paintings dry, display them for everyone to see.

- Students can make fans to cool themselves off. Have them accordion fold sheets of paper, then fold them in the middle and staple the center pieces together. Or have them draw pictures, gluing a tongue depressor between them for a handle. Let them try out their fans in the warm classroom the rest of the day.

Extension Activities

- Have students make hand fans (see page 134), then take them to the residents of a local senior care center. You might want to have students prepare a program to present. Some of them can read what they wrote about the hottest day they can remember (see page 131). Others can read the poems they wrote about hot summer days (page 131). Encourage students to visit with individual residents. The senior citizens will love the visit and will make your students feel special.

⚠ Bring some milk, ice cream and blenders to class and let students make milk shakes to cool off. A little milk and a lot of ice cream can be turned into a tasty way to beat the heat. You might want to also provide some chocolate syrup and even some fruit such as strawberries. Ask a few parents to come, with their blenders, to help. Let your students make a shake for the principal and take it to the office for a nice surprise!

Values Education Experience

- Ask students what they do in the summertime when they don't have anything to do. Do they complain? Pout? Just sit or lie around and wait for something to happen? Discuss the importance of thinking of others, not just ourselves. When they don't have anything to do, students can help their parents or neighbors or a younger sister or brother. Brainstorm things they can do to be useful and helpful. List the ideas on the board and encourage students to try them out this summer.

Follow-Up/Homework Idea

- Challenge students to brainstorm with their families ways to beat the heat. Then they can try some of them out together in the weeks ahead.

Midsummer Learning Day

July 26

Setting the Stage

• Display books of all kinds with paper and pencils around the caption: "Learning Isn't Just for School." Let each student write about something they've learned this summer. Add their papers to the display.

• Construct a semantic web with words your students think of when you say the word *learning*.

Literary Exploration

Bear's Curiousity Book by David Howgrave-Graham
The Don't Give Up Kid & Learning Differences by Jeanne Gehert
Every Kid's Guide to Thinking and Learning by Joy Wilt Berry
Ramona, the Pest by Beverly Cleary
The Value of Learning by Ann Donegan Johnson

Language Experience
• Encourage students to brainstorm as many words as they can that rhyme with *learn*.

Writing Experience
• Students might want to pick one of these story starters to write about:
> My favorite topic to learn about is . . .
> It's important to learn because . . .
> So far in my life I've learned three important things:
> During summer vacation I learn by . . .
> I would like to learn how to . . .

See reproducible on page 141.

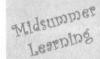

Math Experience

• Involve students in a review of what they have learned about math. Let them work in pairs, taking turns asking each other math questions or provide math problems for them to solve.

Science/Health Experience

• Study how scientists learn new facts and solve problems (read, study, experiment, etc.).

• Talk about concentration. How does concentrating help us learn. How can we learn to concentrate better?

Social Studies Experience

• Discuss learning, including the part listening and focusing play in the learning process.

• Discuss and illustrate helpful study habits such as concentration, alleviating distractions and taking breaks as needed.

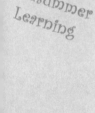

Music/Dramatic Experience

• Let students role-play possible situations that help or hinder their learning. (Example: Trying to study or do work when a neighbor is annoying them.)

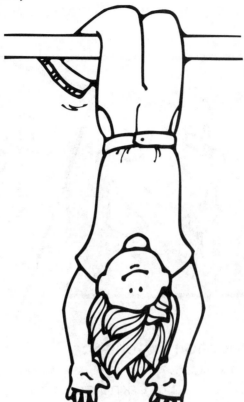

Physical/Sensory Experience

• Ask students to think how they use their different senses to learn. (Example: To learn about a flower they look at it with their eyes, smell it with their noses and touch it with their hands.)

Arts/Crafts Experience

• Students can make small chalkboard slates by gluing wooden frames of craft sticks around black construction paper. They can use chalk to draw pictures, write math problems or write their names on their slates.

Arts/Crafts Experience continued

• Have each student draw a picture of his or her head, then draw symbols inside the head to illustrate what they've learned this year or during the summer. (Examples: tennis racket—how to play tennis, ball—how to play baseball, child—how to baby-sit)

Values Education Experience

• Discuss the value of learning. We never stop learning and growing. Reinforce the idea of asking questions and the joy of discovering new things.

Follow-Up/Homework Idea

• Encourage students to each set up a quiet area with proper lighting at home conducive to studying.

What's in
a Name?

What's in
a Name?

What's in
a Name?

What's in a Name? Day

July 27

Setting the Stage

• Give students name tags to put on their desks. You may prefer to have students make their own name tags.

• Create an interactive center that can be used as a bulletin board later. Draw a picture of a large bicycle with huge wheels and dividing spokes with the caption: "Big Wheels in Our Classroom!" Between each spoke, students can write their names in various categories. (Example: "I like macaroni and cheese" or "I lost my two front teeth.")

• Display a mailbox or a picture of one and envelopes. Add stickers on the envelopes for postage. Each student can write his or her name on an envelope, then put it next to the mailbox. Add the caption: "Our Room Mail Call!"

Setting the Stage continued

- Give each student a wooden clothespin. Explain that it will be for identifying art projects hung on a clothesline throughout the year. Each student can decorate the clothespin and print his or her name on it.

- Do you ever feel like you keep calling on the same people over and over? Solve this problem by labeling craft sticks with student names. Keep them in a container to be used many ways, such as for answering questions or picking a line leader. An added benefit is the suspense involved in students wondering whether their names will be picked. If a student is not paying attention, you can say, "I'm sorry this person is not ready yet," then put the stick back and choose another one. Students will begin paying better attention!

- Construct a semantic web with words your students think of when you say the word *name*.

Literary Exploration

A, My Name Is Alice by Jane Bayer
Andy (That's My Name) by Tomie dePaola
The Boy Who Would Not Say His Name by Elizabeth Vreeken
But Names Will Never Hurt Me by Bernard Waber
Chrysanthemum by Kevin Henkes
Did You Hear the Wind Sing Your Name? by Sandra deCoteau Orie
Don't Call Me Little Bunny by Gregoire Solotareff
Ebbie by Eve Rice
Everyone Wears His Name by Emily Taitz
The Hundredth Name by Shulamith Oppenheim
If You Call My Name by Crescent Dragonwagon
I Hate My Name by Eva H. Grant
I Never Knew Your Name by Sherry Garland
Jessica by Kevin Henkes
Josephina Hates Her Name by Diana Engel
The Man Whose Name Was Not Thomas by N. Jean Craig
Mommy Doesn't Know My Name by Suzanne Williams
My Name Is Bert by Justine Korman
My Name Is Ernie by Tish Rabe
My Name Is Grover by Tish Rabe
No-Name Dog by Rose Impey
The Other Emily by Gibbs Davis
A Porcupine Named Fluffy by Lester
Sabrina by Martha Alexander
Small Bear's Name Hunt by Adelaide Holl
Trouble Is His Name by Elizabeth R. Montgomery
What's Your Name? by Scott Peterson
Why Did They Name It? by Hannah Campbell

What's in a Name?

My name is:
Jessica

What's in a Name?

My name is:
Jessica

What's in a Name?

144

Language Experience

• Write students' names on individual cards. Let them practice alphabetizing the names or matching the names with the same vowel sounds.

Writing Experience

• Students can write what they would like to be named if they were given a choice. They should explain the reasons for their choices.

• Have students write acrostic poems using the letters in their names. Encourage them to think of positive attributes to describe themselves. (Example: DAN—Determined, Athletic, Nice)

• Let students write limericks using their names.
Example:
    There once was a boy named Matt
    Who never looked when he sat
    He did so again,
    Never realizing that when
    He sat down it was on a fat cat!

See reproducible on page 150.

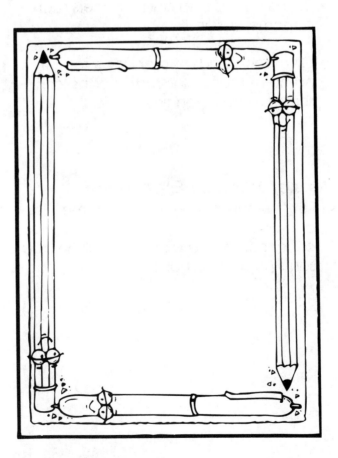

Math Experience

• Let students figure out how much their names are worth. Assign each letter of the alphabet a numerical value. (Example: "A = $1, B = $2" and so on.) Who has the most expensive name? Whose name costs the least?

• Have students print, then measure their names in inches and centimeters.

Science/Health Experience

• Play a fun game of What's My Invention? Give students a list of inventors or scientists whose names are involved in their invention. Students guess what each person's invention or discovery was. (Examples: Louis Braille—Braille alphabet, Levi Strauss— Levi jeans, Henry Ford—Ford car, Sylvester Graham—Graham crackers.)

Graham crackers?

Social Studies Experience

• Review good and bad manners such as name-calling.

• Give each student a chance to name as many classmates as he or she can in a given time period.

Music/Dramatic Experience

• Let students play a musical game! They sing, "My name is _____ and I like to _____ (students fill in blanks). After everyone sings his or her name and a hobby, call on students to each sing another person's name and hobby. This is a good test of memory!

Physical/Sensory Experience

- Play Call Ball! Students sit in a circle or square and toss a rubber or foam ball to one another. Each time the ball is tossed, the one tossing must say the name of the student to whom the ball is thrown. This is a good way for students to learn one another's names.

- Let students play a game of Red Rover. Divide the class into two teams facing each other across a playing area. Each side locks hands tightly. One team picks a person from the other side and chants, "Red Rover, Red Rover, send _____ (name) right over." That person lets go of his neighbors' hands and runs to the other side, trying to break through the locked hands. If successful, he gets to pick someone to take back to his team. If he cannot break through the human chain, he has to stay with that team. The team that gets the most players wins.

Red Rover, Red Rover, send Charlie right over!!!

My name is: Jessica

What's in a Name?

My name is: Jessica

What's in a Name?

My name is: Jessica

What's in a Name?

Arts/Crafts Experience

• Let each student write his or her name in clear printing or cursive, trying to create an animal, insect or object out of it. Students can put their work in a common pile. Students take turns picking a name, at random to figure them out.

• Students can create Name Blottos! Let them paint their names in thick tempera paint, each on one side of a sheet of paper. Then they fold their papers in half and press gently, leaving an imprint on the other half of the sheet. Reinforce the idea of symmetry with this activity.

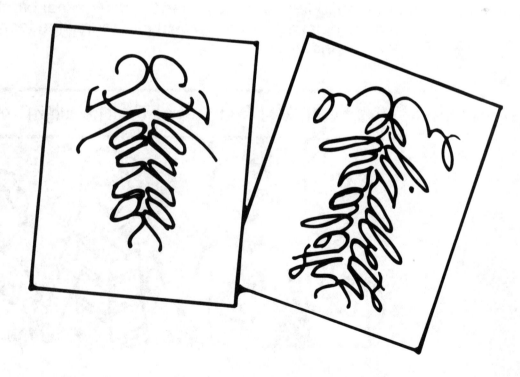

Arts/Crafts Experience continued

- Students enjoy making designs with their names. Why not make an art project out of it? Have them write their names in neat print or cursive, then outline them several times. They can use markers or crayons to fill in the outlines with various colors and designs.

Extension Activities

⚠ Students can write their names on crackers with liquid cheese or squeeze frosting on graham crackers for fun snacks!

Values Education Experience

- Talk about an "honorable name" because of good behavior and actions.

Follow-Up/Homework Idea

- Students can ask their parents why they were given the names they have.

TLC10485 Copyright © Teaching & Learning Company, Carthage, IL 62321-0010

My name is: Jessica

What's in a Name?

My name is: Jessica

What's in a Name?

My name is: Jessica

What's in a Name?

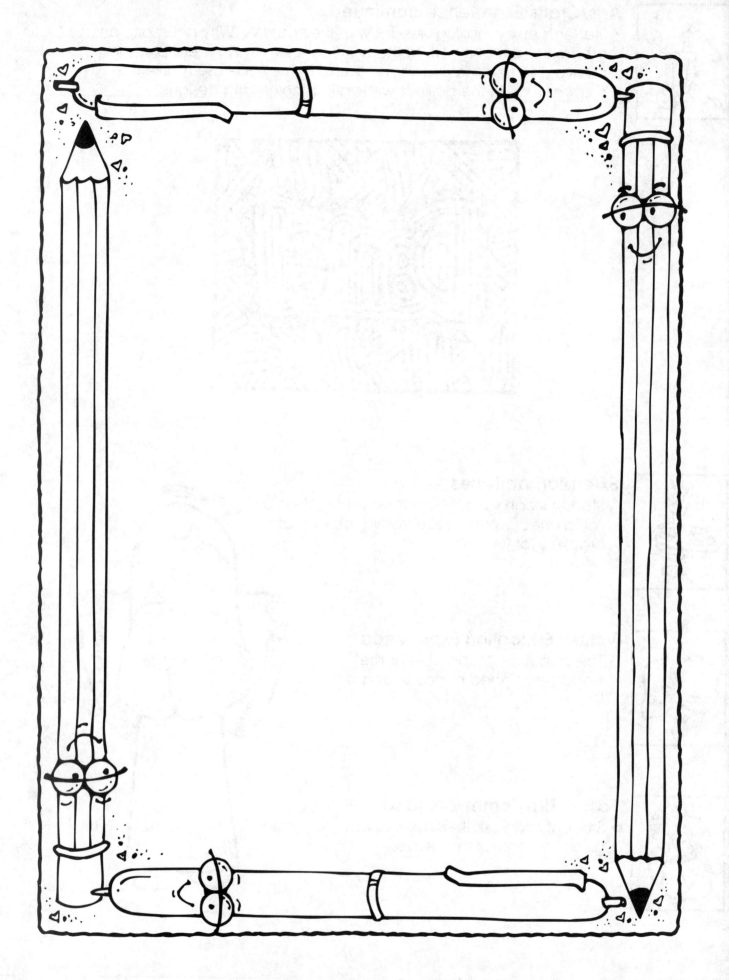

150

Beatrix Potter's Birthday

July 28

Setting the Stage
- Display Beatrix Potter books around stuffed animals representing the animal characters she wrote about: bunnies, frogs, mice, kittens, squirrels and ducks.

Historical Background
Children's author, Beatrix Potter, was born on this day in 1866.

Literary Exploration

The ABC Bunny by Wanda Gag
Bad, Bad Bunny Trouble by Hans Wilhelm
The Big Bunny and the Magic Show by Steven Kroll
Bunnies and Their Sports by Nancy Carlson
Bunny Bath by Lena Anderson
Bunny Book by Richard Scarry
Bunny Box by Lena Anderson
Bunny Fun by Lena Anderson
Bunny Rabbit Rebus by David Adler
Bunny Story by Lena Anderson
Bunny Tail by Susan Hall
Bunny Trouble by Hans Wilhelm
Cottontails: Little Rabbits of Field and Forest by Ron Fisher
Funny Bunnies by Edward Thomson
Funny Bunnies on the Run by Robert Quackenbush
Hattie Rabbit (series) by Dick Gackenback
Home for a Bunny by Margaret Wise Brown
The Hungry Little Bunny by Irma Wilde
I Love You Bunny Rabbit by Shulamith Oppenheim
The Life of a Rabbit by Jan Feder
Little Bunny (series) by Ulf Nilsson
Little Rabbit Foo Foo by Michael Rosen
Little Rabbit's Baby Brother by Fran Manushkin
Little White Rabbit by Edith Oswald
My Hopping Bunny by Robert Bright
Rabbit Garden by Miska Miles
The Rabbit Garden by Georgia Tufts
Rabbits by Fiona Henrie
Rabbits, All About Them by Alvin and Virginia Silverstein
The Runaway Bunny by Margaret Wise Brown
Taking Care of Your Rabbit by Joyce Pope
Tale of Benjamin Bunny by Beatrix Potter
Tale of Peter Rabbit and Other Stories by Beatrix Potter
The World of Peter Rabbit and Friends by Beatrix Potter
The World of Rabbits by Jennifer Coldrey

Language Experience

• Gather your students under the shade of a tree and read one of Beatrix Potter's books to them.

Writing Experience

- Let students write bunny "tales." Provide bunny patterns for them to write their stories on. They can cut out the ears and put them at the top, then attach a cotton ball at the bottom for a tail! See pattern on page 157.

Science/Health Experience

- Study rabbits and their habitat. Ask if any of your students have ever had a pet rabbit? Let them answer class questions about it.

Social Studies Experience

- Have students research Beatrix Potter, then share the information with the rest of the class.

- Let students locate Beatrix Potter's home on a world map.

Music/Dramatic Experience

• Teach your students the song, "Little Bunny Foo Foo."

Physical/Sensory Experience

• Borrow "The Bunny Hop" from the library. Have students form a line with their hands on the waist of those in front of them and do the Bunny Hop together!

Arts/Crafts Experience

- Students can make small Bunny Banks from their lunch milk cartons. They cover one side with a piece of white art paper, stapling it over the top ends and the bottom. They can draw a rabbit face with ears on the paper, trimming it to fit. Pink felt glued on the ear linings and a bow tie on the "neck" are finishing touches. Students can cut a slot on the other side in which to drop their coins.

- Make bunny ears for younger students. Fold an 11" x 14" sheet of paper. Trim off 1 1/2" off the top, leaving a folded square 7" x 7". Fold the square into fourths and draw the outline of one bunny ear in the upper left-hand corner. Cut both pieces, cutting on the fold but not cutting past the folded lines. Bring the paper under the ears forward (sides A and B) and glue them together. Glue flap C over the seam of A and B. Attach string to tie under the child's chin. Let students glue cotton balls on the ears to make them look real!

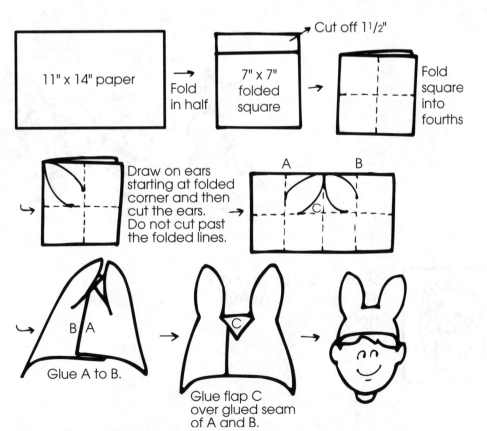

11" x 14" paper → Fold in half → 7" x 7" folded square → Cut off 1 1/2" → Fold square into fourths

Draw on ears starting at folded corner and then cut the ears. Do not cut past the folded lines.

A   B
C

Glue A to B.

Glue flap C over glued seam of A and B.

Extension Activities

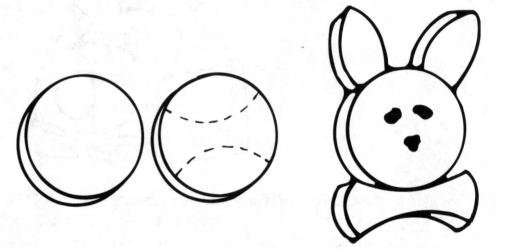

- Invite someone who raises rabbits to visit your class, or take students on a field trip to see where rabbits are raised.

⚠ Make Bunny Biscuits! Give each student two biscuits from a can of refrigerator biscuits. Students can add raisins for the bunny face features on one biscuit. They cut the remaining biscuit as shown below, shaping the pieces into bunny ears and a bow tie. Bake the biscuits according to package directions.

⚠ Host a Beatrix Potter Tea Party. Let students bring favorite stuffed bunnies or other animals. Serve punch and cookies.

Follow-Up/Homework Idea

- Encourage students to check out Beatrix Potter books to read at home.

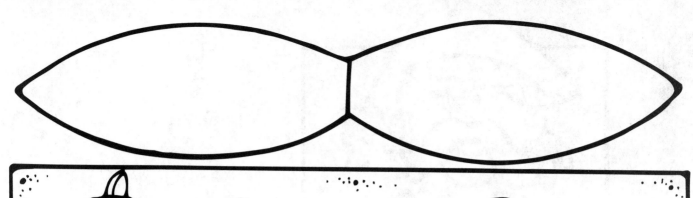

Bunny Tales!

Glue
cotton
here.

Pirate Mania Day

July 29

Setting the Stage

- Display pirate "treasure" (costume jewelry in a box or chest) on a table. Add foil-covered chocolate coins. You can even scatter a few throughout the room. Ahoy, mates!

- Dress like a pirate to greet your class: an eye patch, one earring, a fake moustache, a bandanna, maybe even a hook hanging out of one shirt sleeve! Make pirate pants by cutting an old pair of jeans into raggedy cutoffs, sewing a few patches here and there, then tying a red sash around your waist. Add a striped T-shirt and you're all set!

Pirate Mania

Pirate Mania

Pirate Mania

Setting the Stage continued

- Arrange your room for cooperative groups. Divide the class into groups and let each group name their "pirate ship" and design a ship's flag. The flags may be taped onto rulers and secured in the center of each group of desks. Groups can work together throughout the day on projects, earning "pirate points" by working well together. This will help with classroom management and ensure that "all hands are on deck!"

- Give students an opportunity to tell you all that they already know about pirates. Write this up in the form of a semantic map or web. Then ask them to list questions they have about pirates to help you structure the course of the day.

Historical Background

Blackbeard was a pirate whose real name was Edward Teach. He loved to terrify prisoners by putting burning rope inside his beard. His beard was greasy and long. He wiped his hands on it after eating his meals. Blackbeard and other pirates roamed the seas laying in wait for treasure-filled merchant ships. Shiver me timbers!

Literary Exploration

Alvin the Pirate by Ulf Lofgren

Are You Pirates? by Steven Kroll

Captain Abdul's Pirate School by Colin McNaughton

"Captain Blackbeard Did What?" and "Captain Hook" poems from
   Shel Silverstein's *Light in the Attic* and *Where the Sidewalk Ends*

Come Away from the Water, Shirley by John Burningham

The Forgetful Pirate by Leonard Kessler

The Gift of the Pirate Queen by Grania O'Malley

Grandma and the Pirate by David Lloyd

I Wish I Had a Pirate Suit by Pamela Allen

Juju and the Pirate by Louis Baum

The Kettleship Pirates by Rodney Pepe

Maggie and the Pirate by Ezra Jack Keats

The Man Whose Mother Was a Pirate by Margaret Mahy

Maybe It's a Pirate by Judy Hindley

Mrs. Pirate by Nick Sharrat

Pearl's Pirates by Frank Asch

Pigwig and the Pirates by John Dyke

Pirate, Pirate, over the Salt, Salt Sea by Patty Wolcott

The Pirate Queen by Marianne MacDonald

The Pirates of Bedford Street by Rachel Isadora

The Pirate Who Tried to Capture the Moon by Dennis Haseley

Pugwash and the Ghost Ship by John Ryan

Sir Francis Drake: His Daring Deeds by Roy Gerrard

Smallest Pirate by Denise Trez

(Older readers may enjoy Barrie's *Peter Pan* or Robert Louis Stevenson's
   Treasure Island or even *The Legend of Blackbeard*).

Language Experience

• Create a Venn diagram together, depicting the similarities and
   differences between pirates and other types of thieves (bank robbers,
   house burglars and old-fashioned train robbers).

Pirate Mania

Pirate Mania

Pirate Mania

160

Writing Experience

• Ask students to imagine a pirate ship is in need of additional crew members. Let them write out job applications highlighting their pirate skills, telling why they should each get the job as the newest pirate!

• Students can write letters to Captain Hook, asking questions about his hook and about how he made adjustments to help him do his daily activities with one hand and one hook. Remind students that this is a fictional letter. In a real-life situation, such a letter might be offensive, insensitive or hurtful.

• To be a pirate in the 1600s, a man had to give up his allegiance to his own country and never go home again. Let students write their feelings about such a choice. See reproducible on page 167.

Math Experience
- Give students gold paper coins to practice counting, addition and subtraction skills with these as math manipulatives. Copy the patterns on gold cardstock. See patterns on page 168.

- If there is a sandy "digging" area in the school yard, take your class there with a portable scale and spoons, cups and various sizes of plastic containers to experiment with measurement.

Science/Health Experience
- Discuss the lack of personal hygiene among most pirates. How would such a lack of cleanliness affect one's health? Talk about germs. Also discuss the limited diet of pirates as they spent most of their time at sea with no fresh fruits or vegetables. Have students find out about rickets, a common malady of seamen.

162

Social Studies Experience

• Let students research pirates who became famous in history: Blackbeard, Jolly Roger, Captain Hook, Long John Silver, Mary Read, etc.

• Review mapmaking skills with buried treasure maps. Let students form cooperative groups. Get permission for them to hide shoe boxes of "treasures" (pencils, coins, erasers) around the school. Then have them make treasure maps on large paper sacks. They tear each sack in a large rectangular square, crumple it, then wet it all over. They smooth out the map while still wet, then let it dry. They can draw their maps with colored chalk for an authentic look. Let the groups exchange maps and try to find the buried treasure!

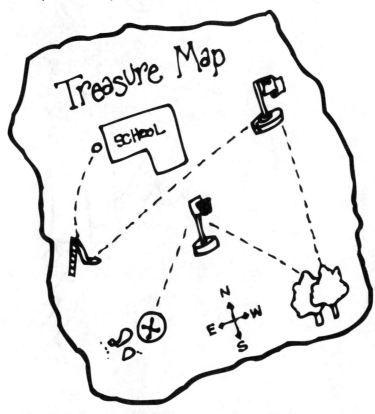

Music/Dramatic Experience

• Let students have some fun with dramatic play as pirates! Provide banana "swords" or, if the weather is warm, use water squirt guns!

Pirate Mania

Physical/Sensory Experience

- Play Hit the Deck! Have students line up on one side of the gym. Choose a student to be lead pirate. When the lead pirate says "Attack!" everyone runs toward a goal. When the lead pirate says "Retreat!" students turn around and run back to where they started. When the lead pirate says "Hit the deck," students fall to the floor. The student who gets to the goal first wins.

- Let students pretend to "walk the plank" on a balance beam from gym class to improve gross motor coordination skills.

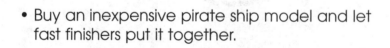

- Buy an inexpensive pirate ship model and let fast finishers put it together.

- If you have a pole on your school playground, let students try to "climb the mast" to check for possible intruders into your pirate paradise!

164

Arts/Crafts Experience

- Provide black construction paper and an eye patch pattern for students to make. They can wear them throughout the day. See patterns on page 169.

Fold over, insert string and glue.

- Let students decorate their own treasure boxes to take home to put their treasures in. They can bring boxes with lids (shoe boxes, gift boxes) from home. Have them paint or cover the boxes with paper. They can use patterns and gold cardstock to make "brass" locks and corners. See patterns on page 170.

Extension Activities

⚠ Make pirate ship treats: apple wedge pirate ships with cheese triangle sails on toothpick masts.

⚠ Let students dig for "buried treasure." "Bury" Oreo™ cookies in clear plastic cups filled with chocolate pudding (dirt).

Extension Activities

⚠ Serve chocolate eclair "pirate ships." Place eclairs in clear, plastic banana boat dishes, each with a drinking straw mast holding a pirate symbol (skull and crossbones) paper sail. See flag patterns on page 171.

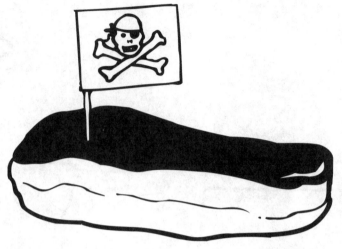

⚠ Have a Pirate Picnic! Seat students in a grassy area and serve hoagie sandwiches, root beer and "pirate peg leg pretzels!"

⚠ Students will enjoy Edible Treasure Chests. Make a horizontal slice partway through the top of a cupcake. Slip a foil-covered chocolate coin into the sliced part with the coin barely showing. Make one for each student so they can "dig up" the treasure, then eat the cupcake.

Values Education Experience

• What is "treasure" to your students? In other words, what do they value?

Follow-Up/Homework Idea

• Remind students to wash up before and after they eat. Nobody wants to be a "dirty" pirate!

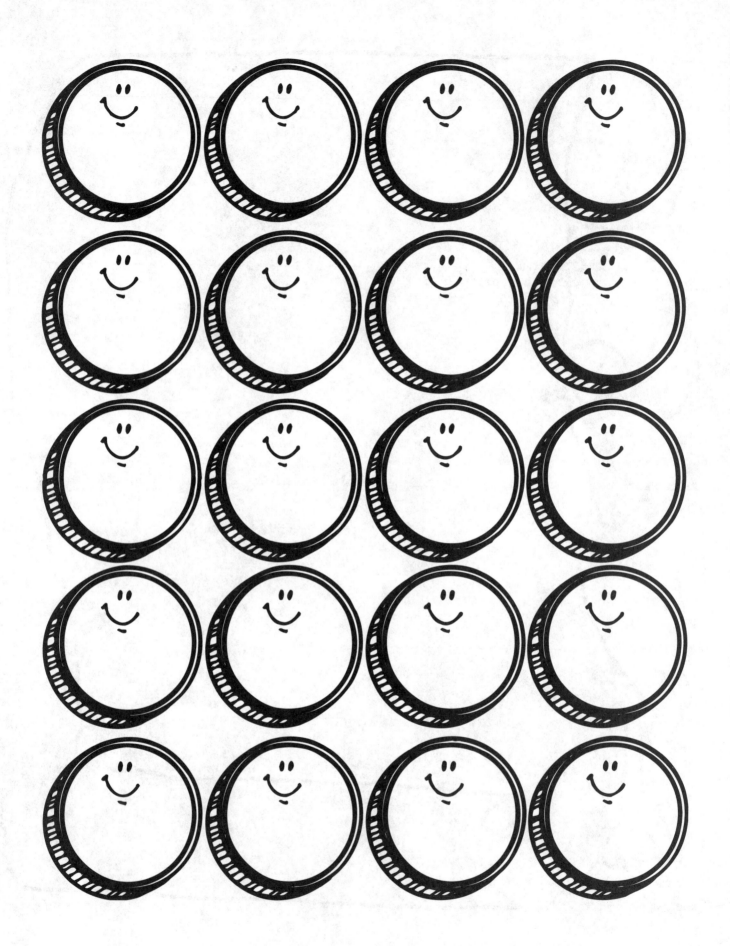

168

Fold over, insert string and glue.

Fold over, insert string and glue.

Fold over, insert string and glue.

Glue to lid side

Glue to corners of box

Glue to box side

Gone Fishin' Day

July 30

Setting the Stage

• Do your students know that fish swim in schools? Explain that your class will be able to go to "school" with the fish today and learn all about them! Display fish pictures and toy fish with a tackle box and a fishing pole with related literature to use as "bait" to get your students "hooked, hook, line and sinker" into today's activities!

• Borrow an aquarium or fishbowl of tropical fish for the day. Students can make observations about a day in the life of a fish.

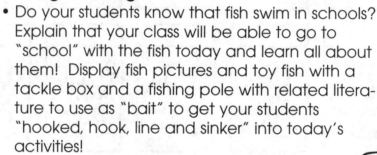

• Mount fish shapes against a blue cellophane or butcher paper background on a bulletin board. Add book jackets and one of these captions: "Get Hooked on a New Book," "Reel One In!" "What a Catch!" or "Fishing for a New Book!"

• Construct a semantic web or map with facts your students know (or would like to know) about fishing.

172

Historical Background

The Chesapeake Bay Bridge opened on this day in 1952. The Chesapeake Bay area is a popular fishing spot, but the United States is filled with lakes, rivers, oceans, streams and ponds where fishermen (and fisherwomen) can catch all kinds of fish. It's one of America's favorite outdoor sports!

Literary Exploration

Curious George Goes Fishing by H.A. Rey
Elizabeth Catches a Fish by Jane Resh Thomas
Fish by Martin Andrews
The Fish Book by Dick Martin
The Fisherman and His Wife by Jacob Grimm
Fish Eyes: A Book You Can Count On by Lois Ehlert
Fish, Fish, Fish by Georgie Adams
Fish for Supper by M.B. Goffstein
Fish Fry by Susan Saunders
Fish Fry Tonight by Jackie Koller
A Fish in His Pocket by Denys Cazet
Fish Is Fish by Leo Lionni
A Fish Out of Water by Helen Palmer
Fish Story by Katharine Andres
The Fish That Wasn't by Paul Borovsky
I Did It! by Harlow Rockwell
I Want to Be a Fisherman by Carla Greene
Let's Catch a Fish by Jack Stokes
Little Black Fish by Samuel Bahrang
The Little Fish That Got Away by Bernadine Cook
Loudmouth George and the Fishing Trip by Nancy Carlson
McElligot's Pool by Dr. Suess
A Million Fish . . . More or Less by Patricia McKissack
One Fish, Two Fish, Red Fish, Blue Fish by Dr. Suess
One Small Fish by Joanne Ryder
A Patchwork Fish Tale by Stewart Moskowitz
Rainbow Fish by Marcus Pfister
Swimmy by Leo Lionni
That's Not a Fish! by Tony Bradman
Tobias Catches a Trout by Ole Hertz
Trout the Magnificent by Sheila Turnage

Gone Fishin'

Gone Fishin'

Gone Fishin'

Gone Fishin'

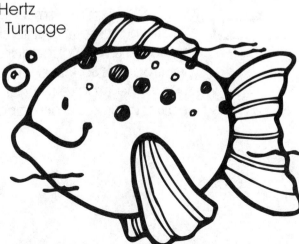

Language Experience

• Let students brainstorm words that rhyme with *fish*.

Writing Experience

• Let students write tall tales about fish they almost caught! They can write on fish shapes, then display them on a bulletin board entitled "Fish Tales." See pattern on page 180.

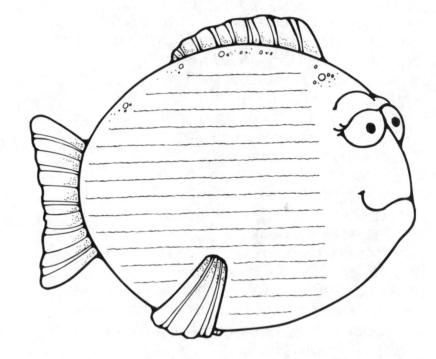

Math Experience

• Let students make counting books for younger students patterned after Lois Ehlert's *Fish Eyes: A Book You Can Count On.*

⚠ Students can use small fish crackers as math manipulatives for counting, addition and subtraction practice. Provide fish crackers in various flavors (cheddar, onion, sour cream, pretzel and original), and let students sort and graph them according to color and/or flavor. Serve the crackers on blue napkins (for water) and provide extra napkins for keeping hands clean.

Math Experience continued

- Explain to students that fishermen can keep only fish that are a certain length. This assumes that young fish will survive to repopulate the area. Post an authentic-looking sign that gives the minimum measurement requirement. Let students measure various lengths of paper fish (in inches or centimeters) to see whether they are "keepers" or if they have to be thrown back in the water. Lay a circle of blue paper on the floor for the "throw backs." See patterns on page 181.

See patterns on page 181.

Science/Health Experience

- Study fish and their habitats. What sea creatures are not classified as "fish"?

Social Studies Experience

- Have students locate on a map places around the country with lakes, rivers or oceans that might be good "fishing holes."

- Study the fishing industry in North America. What parts of the continent have the most professional fishing?

Music/Dramatic Experience

- Students can cut fish shapes from construction paper, then write their favorite songs on them. They can attach a small piece of magnetic tape to each fish. Provide wooden dowels with strings attached for fishing poles. Attach a magnet on the string. Place the fish shapes with songs on them on the floor in a pile (fishing hole). Let students go fishing for songs to sing! (This game can also be adapted for letter or vowel sounds, high-frequency words or favorite finger plays.) See patterns on page 182.

- Create a class "fish tale." Begin a fishing story, then "cast" a spool of fishing line (or thread) to a student who adds to the story. After a minute that student "casts" the fishing line to someone else to continue the story. The last students must finish the tale.

Physical/Sensory Experience

- Bring a small wading pool and a toy fishing pole to class. Put a little water in the pool and add plastic fish. Let students practice casting and reeling in fish. Or let younger students use a minnow net to scoop up the fish.

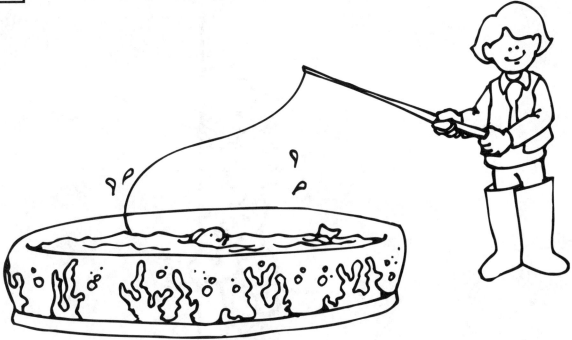

- Students can also "blow" for fish. They cut fish shapes from colored tissue paper and scatter them on a table. They inhale through a drinking straw, to "catch" as many fish as they can!

Physical/Sensory Experience continued

• Play a game of Sardines! One child is "It." The other children count to 100 very slowly, keeping their eyes closed while "It" hides. When the others finish counting, they shout, "Ready or not; here we come!" When someone finds "It," he or she hides with "It." The game is over when everyone is hiding in the same place with "It!"

Arts/Crafts Experience

• Read Marcus Pfister's *Rainbow Fish* book. Then let students create their own colorful fish, painting in beautiful, vivid colors and sprinkling glitter on them before the paint dries. See patterns on page 183.

178

Arts/Crafts Experience continued

- Help younger students cut a triangle from the side of a paper plate, then secure it to the plate to make an easy fish. They can paint scales and a fin and glue on a wiggly eye.

- Let students paint various kinds and colors of fish on white art paper. While the paint is drying, they can make crayon shavings with the blunt end of scissors. They cut out their fish and arrange the colored shavings on wax paper. Then they cut another piece of wax paper to fit over the first piece. An adult can help by pressing a warm iron on the wax paper with crayon shavings and fish inside. The colors will melt and bleed together to create a beautiful picture. A fishbowl "frame" can be cut out to put around the wax paper image. Hang the fish in class windows for a stained glass effect.

  Caution! Supervision required. Be extremely careful when using the iron!

Extension Activities

⚠ Put Swedish Fish™ (like Gummy Worms™) candies in raspberry-blue gelatin for a fun treat. Sardines on crackers is an easy alternative.

Follow-Up/Homework Idea

⚠ Students can ask their parents to let them make tuna salad sandwiches for the family tonight.

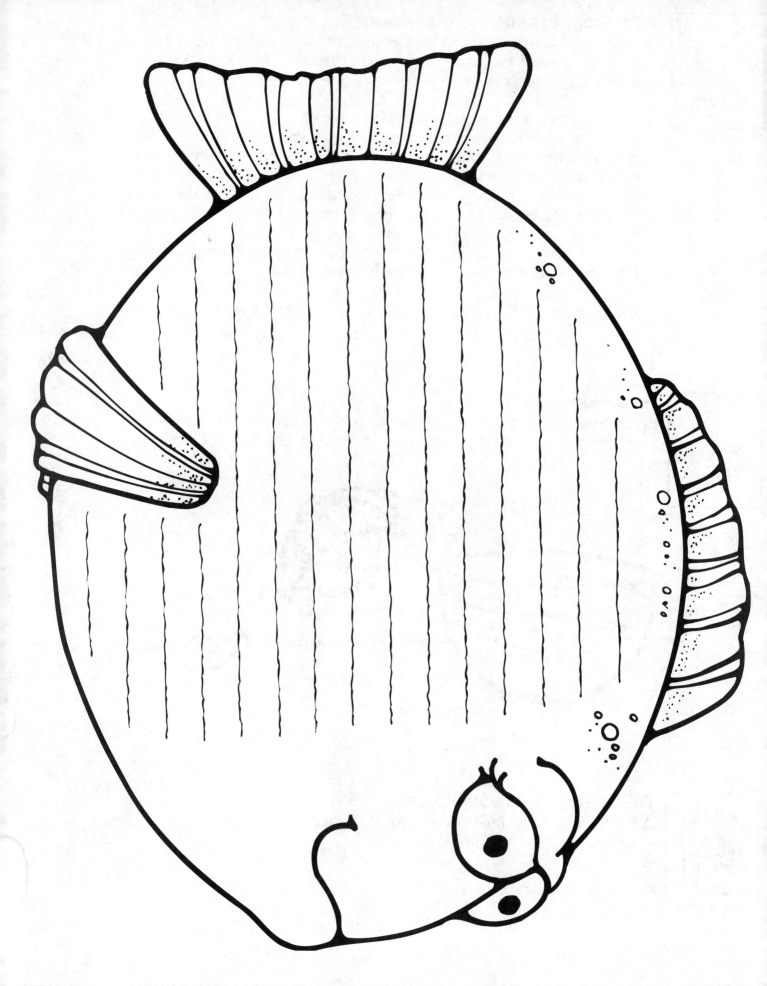

180

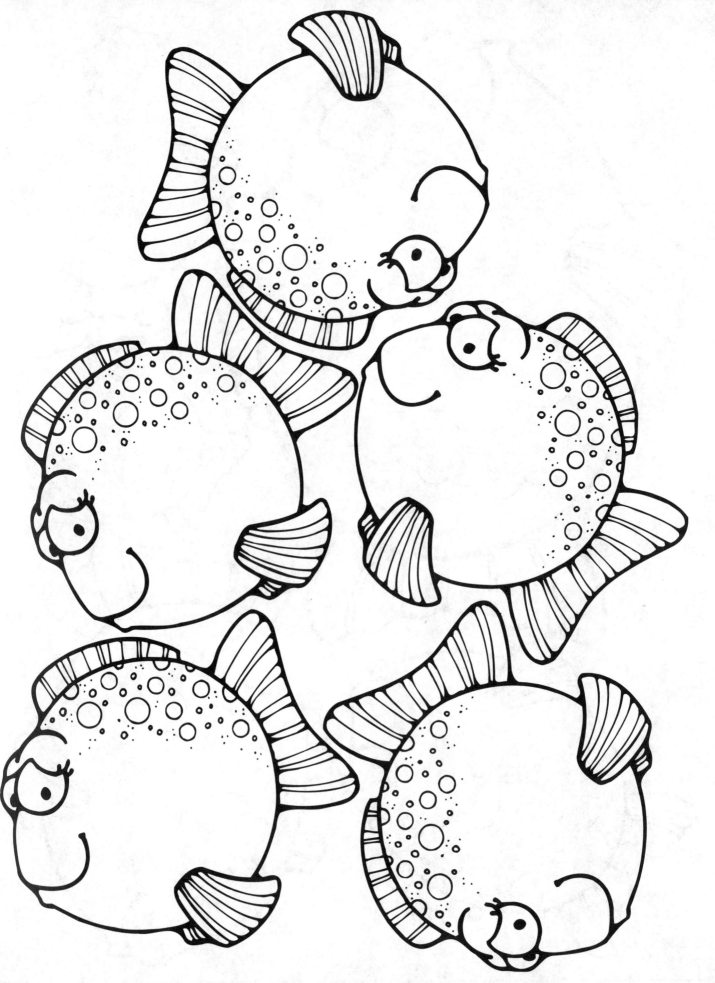

182

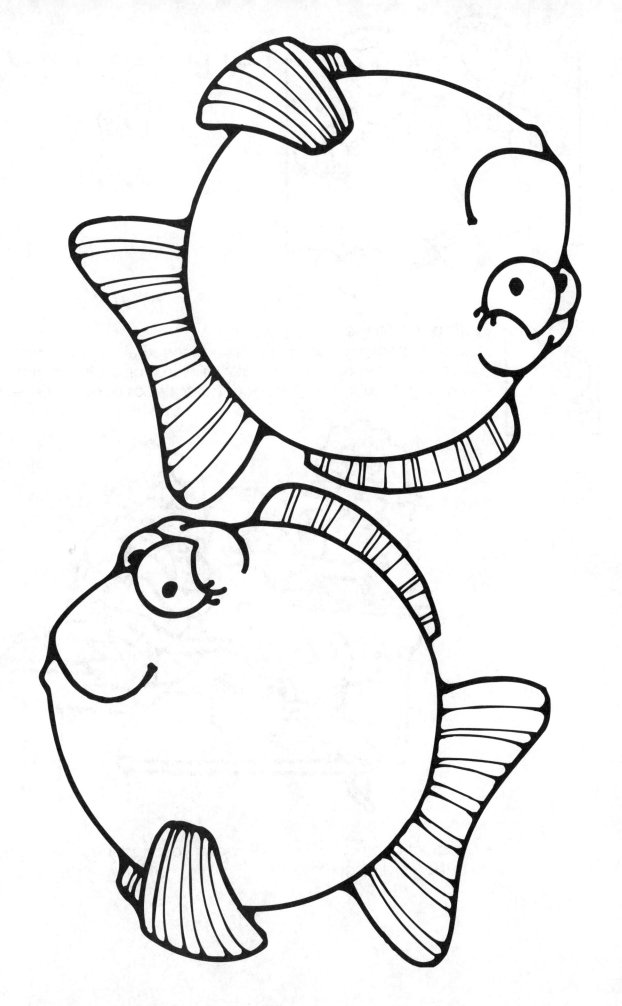

Gingerbread Day

July 31

Setting the Stage

• Let a simmering potpourri pot provide the smell of ginger spice so your students smell it as they walk into the room. Explain that today they will be making gingerbread that tastes as good as it smells!

• Construct a semantic web with words your students think of when you say the word *gingerbread*.

Literary Exploration

Ben's Gingerbread Man by Niki Daly
The Gingerbread Boy by Paul Galdone
The Gingerbread Boy by Harriet Ziefert
The Gingerbread Doll by Susan Tews
The Gingerbread Man by Sally Claster Bell
The Gingerbread Man by Eric Kimmel
The Little Gingerbread Man by Fran Hunia
Snipp, Snapp, Snurr and the Gingerbread Man by Maj. Lindman

Language Experience

• Let students review the sequence of events in *The Gingerbread Man* story. They can write these main events on accordion-folded gingerbread man cutouts. (Help them cut out the figures, being sure not to cut across the fold so they stay connected.)

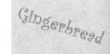

• Have students brainstorm words to describe the gingerbread man in the story (fun-loving, independent, joyful, naughty, etc.).

Writing Experience

• Let students write their own stories about foods that suddenly come to life and act like people.

• Students can write their own endings to the story of the gingerbread man. (Examples: He goes to live in a gingerbread house; he gets married to a gingerbread girl and raises little cookies; he runs off to Hollywood and becomes a star.)

Writing Experience continued

• Challenge students to write newspaper stories with headlines, reporting on a gingerbread man gone bad, a tough cookie on a crime spree. Encourage them to use humor in their stories.

Gingerbread

Math Experience

• Let students cut out several gingerbread house shapes from card-stock. They can each write a number on the roof. Show them how to section off the rest of the house in three or four pieces (like puzzle pieces). On each section they write a math problem whose answer is on the roof. (Example: 5 on the roof = 3 + 2, 10 - 5, 0 + 5 or 8 - 3.) Students cut the house puzzle pieces apart and put them in a class pile. Then they trade roofs with one another. The goal is to find the puzzle pieces that go with their roofs and assemble the houses. See patterns on page 189.

Gingerbread

• Enlarge the gingerbread recipe on page 188 so everyone can see it or give a copy to each student. Have them use their math skills to double and/or triple the recipe.

Gingerbread

Science/Health Experience

• Study ginger—how it grows, what the rhizome looks like, how it smells, what its health benefits are, where it comes from, etc. If possible, bring a ginger rhizome to class for students to see.

Music/Dramatic Experience

• Let your students act out *The Little Gingerbread Man* story.

Physical/Sensory Experience

• Students form a circle that becomes the "home" of the little old man and woman. One student is chosen to be the gingerbread man. Others take turns being the old man and the old woman chasing the gingerbread man around the circle until they catch him or the door (a designated opening in the circle) opens and lets the gingerbread man out.

Arts/Crafts Experience

• Students can make gingerbread boy and girl puppets. They cut out patterns and glue them on paper lunch bags. Then they chant "Run, run as fast as you can. You can't catch me. I'm the Gingerbread Man!" They make their puppets "talk" as they chant. See patterns for boy and girl on pages 190-191.

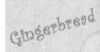

Extension Activities

⚠ For a little added fun today, bring a giant gingerbread man to class. Make gingerbread cookie dough (recipe below) into the form of a giant boy before class. Then bake it according to directions. Put it in a hidden place to cool. Then take your students to the oven to find that your gingerbread man is missing and all that's left is a note that says, "Run, run as fast as you can. You can't catch me. I'm the gingerbread man!" Begin a search for the missing gingerbread man! Finally, have someone come to your class excitedly expressing his or her relief at finding the lost Gingerbread Man. Serve the giant cookie to your students for a yummy, well-earned treat!

Gingerbread Cookies

2/3 c. shortening
1 c. sugar
2 T. molasses
2 eggs
2 T. milk with 1 t. lemon juice
1 t. soda
3 c. flour
1 t. salt
1 t. baking powder
1 t. cinnamon
1 1/2 t. ginger

Cream shortening and sugar together. Add eggs and molasses to the mixture. Add milk and dry ingredients to above mixture. Mix thoroughly. Roll out dough and shape into cookies. Bake at 375°F for 8-10 minutes.

188

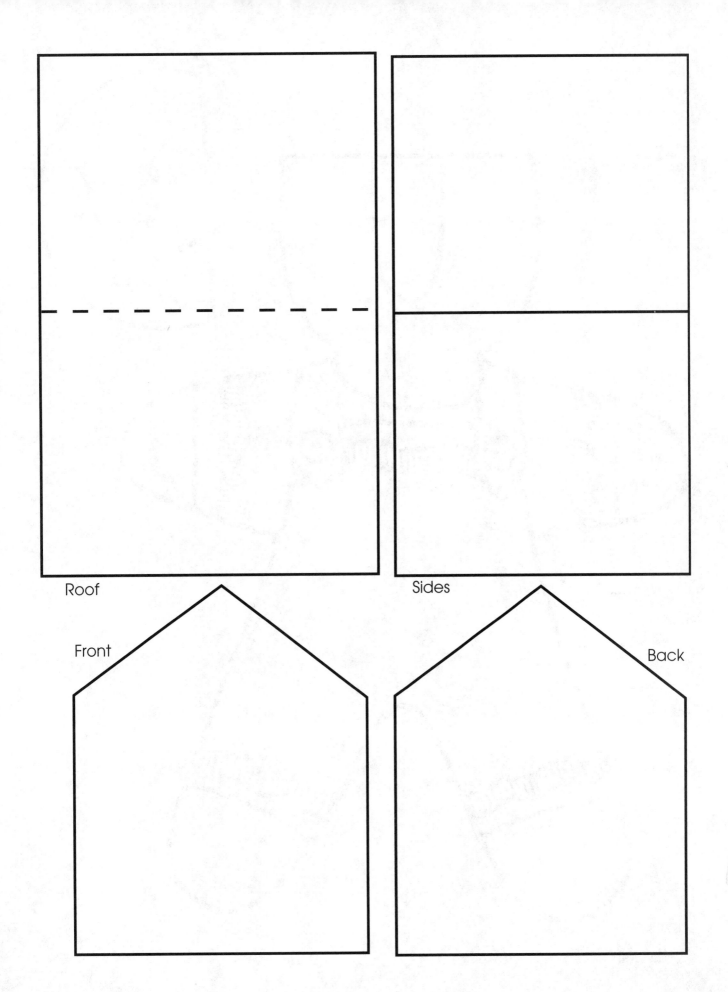

Roof

Sides

Front

Back

190

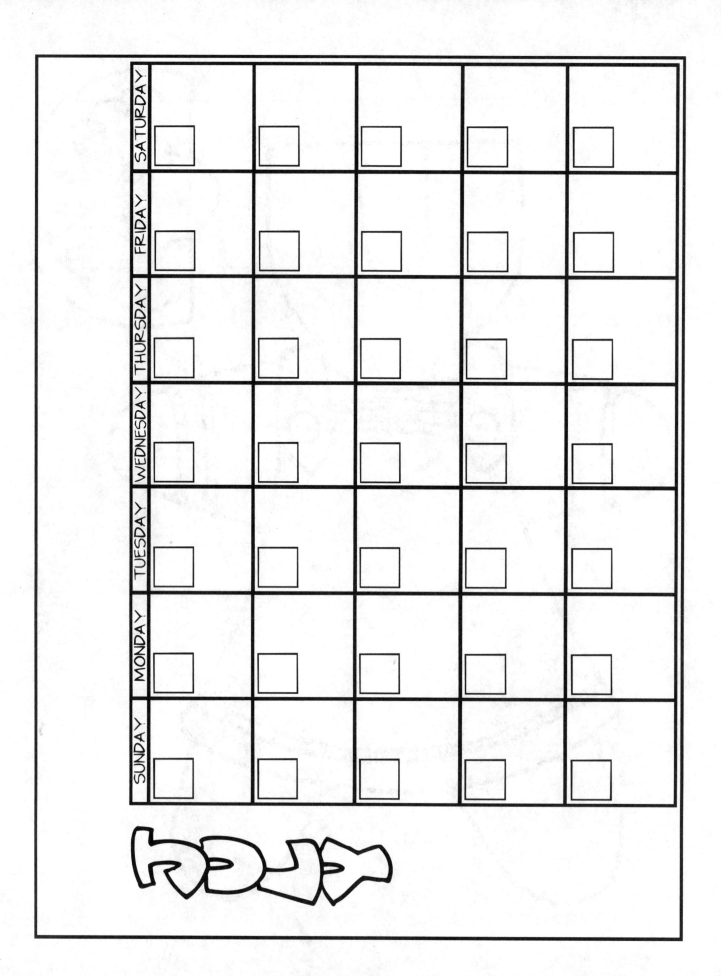